Claire Harrison

START & SCALE your HR business

A practical **guide for HR professionals** to create a successful consulting business and a life with flexibility and purpose

'Using personal experiences and relevant insights, Claire lays out the journey and process to become an HR consultant. The IGNITE stages represent a mindset and the actions to create a thriving consulting business.'
Dave Ulrich, Rensis Likert Professor, Ross School of Business (retired) & Partner, the RBL Group

'I first met Claire when she was pregnant with her first child and working for another HR practice. Over the years, I've had the privilege of working alongside her as she built a thriving HR consulting business while raising a family, which takes determination, courage, and self-belief. I've watched Claire navigate the complexities of business ownership with resilience, professionalism, and a deep commitment to delivering value. She has built Harrisons into a highly successful consulting firm, proving that HR professionals can not only lead but also build and scale their own businesses. *Start & Scale Your HR Business* is the ultimate guide for those ready to take that leap. Claire is the ideal mentor for HR specialists looking for financial independence and control over their careers. Congratulations, Claire, on your success, and I look forward to your influence on a new generation of HR consultants making the world a better place, one workplace at a time.'
Amanda Cole, Managing Director, Spark Consultants

'The world of HR is evolving fast, and more professionals are looking for ways to work differently, on their own terms. In *Start & Scale Your HR Business*, Claire provides a clear, practical roadmap for HR professionals who want to take their expertise beyond corporate roles and build a successful business. With deep industry knowledge and hands-on experience, Claire offers a fresh perspective on what it takes to thrive as an independent HR consultant in today's world of work.'
Lucy Adams, CEO, Disruptive HR

'I've had the privilege of knowing Claire Harrison since our early days navigating the complexities of HR at BHP, and it's been truly inspiring to witness her remarkable evolution into a successful

business owner and a recognised leader in our field. Claire's book, *Start & Scale Your HR Business*, is a testament to her deep industry expertise, and her pragmatic and astute business perspective. It's a brilliant and practical guide for any HR professional ready to embark on their own entrepreneurial journey, providing the kind of real-world insights only someone with Claire's experience can offer.'
Jo Cairns, Chief People & Culture Officer

'I've known Claire for many years, both professionally and personally, and I have always been inspired by her commercial acumen, drive, and especially her ability to balance the demands of running a successful business with juggling family and community commitments. I don't hesitate to refer clients to Claire because I know she combines strategic HR expertise with a strong commercial mindset to drive meaningful business outcomes. Claire has built Harrisons into a thriving consulting business, proving that HR professionals can not only lead but also build and scale their own successful enterprises. *Start & Scale Your HR Business* is a must-have guide for those looking to do the same.'
Christy Miller, Partner, Clayton Utz

'I've had the privilege of watching Claire grow from a young L&D professional to a confident, successful business owner. Her book, *Start & Scale Your HR Business*, is an honest, smart and empowering guide for anyone ready to step into consulting.'
Lindsay Thorrington, Head of Career Management / Principal Consultant

'Claire's story is one of courage, growth, and authenticity – this book shares not only what to do, but how to do it while juggling life, family and business. A heartfelt and smart guide for HR professionals wanting to go out on their own.'
Jodi Ord, Psychologist & Ex-HR Director

'Working closely with Claire, I have witnessed firsthand her passion, resilience, and unwavering commitment to delivering excellence and expertise in HR Consulting. Claire is not just a brilliant entrepreneur; she is an inspiring leader who genuinely cares about the motivations and success of her team and clients. This book reflects her deep knowledge, hard-earned lessons, and the generous spirit with which she shares her expertise. For anyone looking to transition from being a 9–5 HR professional to building a thriving, flexible HR Consulting business, there is no better guide than Claire and no better resource than this book.'
Ellissa Lauder, Senior Consultant People & Culture, Harrisons

'Having worked with Claire for several years I can say that her book is a must-read for any entrepreneur looking to navigate the challenges of business with clarity and confidence. Claire's personal experiences, practical frameworks, and actionable insights – like the IGNITE method – offer a valuable roadmap for success. As a recent entrepreneur, I found the book very insightful, so much so that I'm revisiting my own business approach with renewed focus and strategy. I've learnt that modelling those who have already succeeded is one of the best ways to accelerate progress, and I truly appreciate Claire sharing her journey to help others do the same.'
Donna Tomasi, NLP Master Coach, HR and Leadership Consultant

'This book is a game-changer for anyone wanting to turn their HR expertise into a thriving consulting business. Claire Harrison has done an incredible job of distilling everything you need to know – mindset, strategy, marketing, and financials – into one practical and inspiring guide. A must-read for aspiring consultants.'
Andrew Griffiths, International Bestselling Author/Global Speaker

'Claire Harrison's *Start & Scale Your HR Business* is the ultimate roadmap for HR professionals ready to launch or scale their consulting business. Packed with real-world insights, financial

wisdom, and the IGNITE framework, this guide gives you the confidence and tools to succeed – on your terms. A must-read for anyone in HR.'
Dale Beaumont, Founder & CEO of Business Blueprint

'*Start & Scale Your HR Business* is a must-read for HR professionals looking to make the leap into consulting. Claire Harrison shares her wealth of experience with clarity, honesty, and practical insights that make this book both inspiring and actionable. Her IGNITE framework is a game-changer, offering a structured approach to building a sustainable and successful HR business. Whether you're just starting or looking to refine your existing consultancy, this book provides the roadmap you need to thrive. Claire's real-world wisdom, coupled with her step-by-step guidance, makes *Start & Scale Your HR Business* an essential resource for any aspiring HR consultant.'
Suzi Dafnis, CEO, HerBusiness

'I've known Claire for many years; she is a respected industry expert with deep technical HR knowledge and a smart, strategic approach to business. She's built Harrisons into a trusted brand that not only delivers exceptional HR advice but also operates as a high-performing, profitable enterprise. *Start & Scale Your HR Business* is an invaluable guide for HR professionals who want to take control of their careers and build a successful consulting business using proven methodologies that work.'
Deb Richardson, Co-Founder MSQ and Marketing Strategist

'HR and business don't always speak the same language – but Claire bridges that gap effortlessly. She understands how to align people strategy with business success, and she's built an incredible consulting firm in Harrisons that does just that. *Start & Scale Your HR Business* is a goldmine for HR professionals who are ready to take their expertise into the world of business ownership, offering the tools, strategies, and mindset shifts needed to succeed.'
Shona Sherman, Executive Director – People and Operations, HFB Group

Disclaimer
The material in this publication is of the nature of general comment only, and does not represent professional advice. It is not intended to provide specific guidance for particular circumstances and it should not be relied on as the basis for any decision to take action or not take action on any matter which it covers. Readers should obtain professional advice where appropriate, before making any such decision. To the maximum extent permitted by law, the author and publisher disclaim all responsibility and liability to any person, arising directly or indirectly from any person taking or not taking action based on the information in this publication.

WELCOME

Welcome to my book! Thank you for reading.

I'm excited to share my personal journey of building a successful HR business using IGNITE, a framework designed to help you do the same. Whether you're considering leaving your corporate job, seeking better work-life balance, managing family responsibilities or striving for financial freedom, this book is for you. If you've already started your consulting business but aren't seeing the success you hoped for, I'm here to help.

My intention in writing this book is **to help HR professionals transition from employees to business owners with work-life flexibility and financial stability.**

To achieve this intention, I'm sharing my experiences – the highs, lows and lessons learned – hoping they provide inspiration and practical insights. I'm far from perfect and have made many mistakes along the way. Work is just one part of life, and while I strive for balance, I'm not a parenting, health or relationship expert!

This book is a how-to guide of the steps you need to take to become a successful self-employed HR consultant or establish an HR firm with a team. You don't need to read it cover to cover. There is a flow but, like me, there are probably certain topics you're keen to read first. I do recommend starting with the Inspire and Guide sections. You're likely busy, which is why I've included bullet points, checklists, headings, lists and diagrams for an easy read.

Please remember, I'm not offering legal or professional advice here. The guidance in this book is general and based on my own experience. Always consult qualified professionals, such as lawyers and accountants, for your specific circumstances.

Our lives are always a work in progress. Be brave, bold, resilient, positive, and keep moving in the direction you desire. I hope you enjoy and benefit from my book. Please reach out and share your experiences with me.

Enjoy the read.

Claire

For Aileen, David and Linda
xxx

CONTENTS

MY STORY: NOW IS THE TIME TO TAKE THE LEAP

As I reflect on my time as a business owner, there have been incredible highs, daunting lows, and invaluable learnings that have shaped not only my business but me as a person. As I write this book, instead of moving on to my next goal, I'm going to (self-indulgently) practise mindfulness and gratitude by acknowledging and celebrating my years as the Founder and Managing Director of Harrisons.

THE EARLY DAYS: PASSION AND PERSEVERANCE

I started my HR consulting firm, Harrison Human Resources (now named Harrisons) in 2009, the same year my baby girl was born. It was always my dream to run my own business. I loved the idea of being my own boss; with all the accountability, responsibility and supposed flexibility that comes with it.

Six months after my daughter was born, Harrisons was officially launched – albeit very softly – while enjoying my beautiful baby. Starting on my own at home, full of ideas and determination, I plunged into the world of entrepreneurship.

My vision was clear: to create an HR consulting firm that used the best of what I learned in my corporate HR career to help small and medium-sized business (SMBs) owners achieve their goals. I grew up around small business and had empathy for their unique

challenges. I wanted to genuinely understand their needs and help them by providing practical and personalised advice that would empower them as business leaders. After many years in senior corporate HR roles where I felt I wasn't having as much impact as my early years in HR, I sought meaningful work.

The early days were a learning experience on steroids! Sales (it used to be a dirty and scary word), marketing and content writing, writing a business plan, discipline around time management, valuing my time and experience – so much to learn. It was a time of excitement and uncertainty – plus two babies and earning a pittance of my previous corporate salary. Every small win was encouraging, from securing my first client to hiring my first employee, and eventually moving into a "real" office. There were also moments of doubt and struggle. The financial challenges, the long hours and the constant need to prove myself were daunting. Yet, each challenge brought with it a lesson and increased business confidence.

THE HIGHS: CELEBRATING SUCCESSES
Over the years, Harrisons has celebrated numerous successes. We've grown from a micro start-up to a respected HR consulting firm, helping countless businesses achieve their goals. To see the

relief on a new client's face when you're able to solve a problem for them never stops being a fabulous feeling.

Our growth has been consistent, with increased profit year on year. This success is a testament to the hard work, dedication and expertise of the Harrisons team. It's also a reflection of the strong relationships we've built with our clients, who trust Harrisons as their business partner.

Some of my pivotal moments have been:

- the purchase and beautiful fit-out of our own office building
- recruiting a 2IC as Head of Client Services was life-changing for me – and clients and team
- taking a month-long family holiday to Europe while the business ran smoothly – without me
- rebranding from Harrison Human Resources to Harrisons – with our new tagline of People, Purpose, Perform
- the launch of myHRexperts, our online HR membership site
- writing my first book, *The CEO Secret Guide – to managing and motivating employees.*

THE LOWS: LEARNING FROM CHALLENGES

Of course, business ownership hasn't been without its lows.

A challenging aspect for me has always been balancing the demands of running a business with personal commitments. As a wife and mother of two teenagers, finding that equilibrium has sometimes been a struggle. There were and are times when I feel stressed, inadequate and stretched too thin. Every stage of parenting is different; just when you think it may get easier a new challenge arises, from the physically demanding active toddler to the moody and egocentric teenager. And it flies by! And I don't want to miss any of it.

After stress-health issues before Harrisons followed by raising a family, I've come to appreciate the "healthy body, healthy mind" motto. I've had to learn the importance of self-care, compartmentalising, being present in the moment, gratitude and delegation without perfectionism – not to say that I'm perfect at any of it. A fabulous group of supportive and fun friends is exceptionally beneficial. It all helps me manage the juggle of life!

The impact of COVID-19 on all businesses, employers, and employees was profound. The pandemic tested our resilience, forced Harrisons to innovate and pushed us to find new ways to support our clients. In preparation for the anticipated economic downturn, we reduced costs significantly – we moved out of our office, and reduced admin, bookkeeping and marketing costs. And, home schooling! I ran weekly webinars to support our clients, as well as developing and sharing resources about navigating the ever-changing COVID situation at work.

Fortunately for Harrisons, we had new and old clients reaching out for support throughout and post the pandemic. This was a key moment for me – I was worried Harrisons was going to significantly decline. Instead, we were busy making a real difference for businesses and their people; they needed us and that assured me. It helped me move past the scarcity mindset as a business owner, and to have faith that I have built a sustainable business with a strong brand, predictable system of service and loyal client base.

Then there was the Post-COVID Great Resignation and spike in salaries – not a great year for Harrisons on the HR front. We experienced unprecedented consultant turnover and added 20% to our salaries to engage and retain consultants!

GRATITUDE: THANKING THOSE WHO HAVE SUPPORTED US

I am deeply grateful to the many people who have supported Harrisons and me along the way on my business ownership journey.

At Harrisons, I have worked with magnificent people. We're a service business, so without a great team we are unable to deliver a great service to our clients. My team's hard work, client commitment, and support and encouragement of each other has been the backbone of Harrisons' success. #BestTeamBest Business (Harrisons' Vision)

Over the years, I've had a few wonderful business coaches who I have learned so much from. I have worked with one coach in particular on and off for the past eight years – she has been instrumental in keeping me on track with business and life goals. Her guidance has been invaluable.

I am also immensely grateful to my community of fellow business owners who have become an integral part of my support system. Having a group of people who understand and back me and my business because they're in the same boat is priceless. We've supported and encouraged each other through ups and downs, and this has been a source of strength and inspiration.

LOOKING FORWARD: EXCITED FOR THE FUTURE

As I look forward, I am so incredibly excited. As an entrepreneur, I have big plans for Harrisons and new ventures on the horizon for me, including this book. Our purpose of "helping people to make meaningful contributions and connections at work" remains at the core of everything we – and I – do. I remain focused on helping other business owners to build businesses that provide the freedom they seek, just as Harrisons has given me.

I have other exciting projects in the pipeline, including expanding our online HR resources, launching a business start-up program for HR professionals, and further exploring innovative ways to support businesses with AI and other tech tools. Watch this space.

By celebrating my years in business ownership, I hope to encourage others to pursue their entrepreneurial dreams because with passion, perseverance and the right support, anything is possible.

WHY THE TIME IS (RIGHT) NOW

CHAPTER 1

WHY THIS IS THE PERFECT TIME TO START YOUR HR CONSULTING JOURNEY

In a world where remote work, flexibility and the gig economy are our new norm, we are seeking more balance in our life, as well as the ability to take accountability for our work and purpose.

Sadly, there is often a point in your HR career where these expectations cannot be met. Often, we reach a point in our professional HR careers where we need increased flexibility, even simply part-time work, but it is not available. This is crippling to our HR careers as it stagnates our career progression. Not only that, it stifles our professional development and engagement at work if we're not challenged and we're not enjoying our work. But usually we take a lateral move or demotion (with a pay decrease) to balance the needs of work and life.

I see this every day in women wanting to return to work after having children. They are extremely capable but unable to work the long hours required for the next step on the career ladder. Instead, they settle for a lesser job. (And then it is of no surprise that women have significantly less assets and savings than men and as a result, a disproportionate number of women compared to men end up homeless in their later years – but I digress.)

THE POWER OF YOUR EXISTING NETWORK

One of the greatest advantages you bring to starting your HR consulting journey is the network you've already built during your career. After years of working in HR, you've likely developed a wide range of connections – former and current colleagues, fellow HR professionals and key industry contacts. These relationships form a solid foundation for your consulting business. You also have connections with relevant suppliers, such as recruitment agencies, training providers and legal experts, who could become valuable referrers or collaborators as you grow your business.

Beyond this, you "know your stuff" – you have deep expertise in HR, a wealth of practical experience and a proven track record of delivering results. All of these factors position you to hit the ground running, giving you an edge as you launch your consulting practice. Starting your own business isn't about starting from scratch – it's about leveraging what you've already built and applying it in a way that serves your goals and values.

TECHNOLOGY ENABLING REMOTE WORK AND FLEXIBILITY

Enter a surge in technology enabling remote work – our BFF when it comes to work-life flexibility to balance the needs of our professional and personal lives. Thanks to all the online meeting platforms, there is rarely a need, nor an expectation, to physically meet with a client and/or attend a workplace. Saying that, I am a huge fan of teams spending time together at the workplace to increase team communication, collaboration and learning. And the opportunity to get a feel for our client's workplace – and culture – can't be understated.

Other business and work enabling tools such as shared cloud servers and software, CRMs that automate sales and marketing and generative AI to develop content have resulted in business ownership being more affordable and achievable for HR professionals wanting to go solo.

This enables you, as an HR consultant, to easily work remotely with flexibility and deliver great client service.

PEOPLE AND CULTURE ARE DEFINING FACTORS OF ANY ORGANISATION'S SUCCESS

HR is a profession that has significantly evolved from its roots as chaplains and personnel to be a critical function for most organisations (the smart ones). People and culture are *the* defining success factor of any organisation. Without a seat at the table and a comprehensive people strategy, an organisation will never reach its full potential.

As society has changed, so too has the landscape of work and organisations, including employee expectations. The most recent factors that have affected societal and work change are nearly too many to mention but include: longer life span, ageing workforce, generational differences, #metoo, #blacklivesmattter, AI and robotics, LGBTIQ+, feminism, increase in mental health illness, environmentalism, mobile devices and globalisation – plus an increase in the number and complexity of laws that govern our workplaces.

The HR function has become vital in today's world and will continue to gain prominence in the future due to several interconnected trends and challenges that businesses and organisations face, such as the following.

SKILL SHORTAGES

With rapid technological advancements and evolving business needs, attracting, retaining and developing top talent is critical. Skilled employees are a competitive advantage, and HR plays a central role in creating strategies to find and keep the best talent.

WORKPLACE DIVERSITY, EQUITY AND INCLUSION (DEI)

Societal shifts and a growing emphasis on DEI have placed HR at the forefront of ensuring equitable workplace practices. Creating inclusive cultures where everyone feels valued is not only a moral imperative but also enhances innovation, employee engagement and organisational performance.

DIGITAL TRANSFORMATION

As companies embrace AI, automation and other technologies, HR helps manage the human impact of these changes. This includes upskilling employees, fostering digital literacy and supporting staff in adapting to new tools and workflows.

SHIFTING WORKFORCE EXPECTATIONS

Employees today value flexibility, purpose and wellbeing more than ever. The HR function is critical in crafting policies and programs that support hybrid work, mental health initiatives and work-life balance while aligning these efforts with organisational goals.

EMPLOYEE EXPERIENCE AND ENGAGEMENT

In an era where employee experience is as important as customer experience, HR plays a key role in designing and managing the journey of employees within the organisation, from onboarding to development, fostering higher engagement, satisfaction and productivity.

GLOBALISATION AND REMOTE WORK

Businesses operate across borders more than ever, and the rise of remote work has created complex challenges in managing global teams. HR must address cross-cultural dynamics, compliance with varied labour laws and remote team collaboration.

NAVIGATING ECONOMIC AND WORKFORCE UNCERTAINTY

Economic volatility, such as recessions, inflation and industry disruptions, requires agile workforce strategies. HR's role in workforce planning, downsizing, restructuring and re-skilling ensures organisations remain resilient and adaptable.

LEADERSHIP DEVELOPMENT AND SUCCESSION PLANNING

Effective leadership is a top priority for organisations, particularly during times of change. HR is integral to identifying, developing and retaining leaders who can navigate complexity and drive future growth.

THE RISE OF PURPOSE-DRIVEN ORGANISATIONS
Companies with a clear sense of purpose are outperforming others. HR ensures alignment between the organisation's purpose, culture and people strategies, fostering a shared sense of mission and belonging.

THE ETHICAL AND LEGAL COMPLEXITY OF PEOPLE MANAGEMENT
Increased scrutiny on workplace ethics, compliance and governance has made HR a critical function for ensuring organisations adhere to regulations, avoid costly disputes and uphold their reputations.

AI AND PEOPLE ANALYTICS
As AI and analytics transform decision-making, HR's role in leveraging data to make informed decisions about hiring, retention, performance and engagement is becoming more significant.

MENTAL HEALTH AND WELLBEING
Post-pandemic, there's heightened awareness of mental health. HR leads the charge in creating a workplace culture that supports wellbeing through policies, programs and a supportive environment.

SUSTAINABILITY AND SOCIAL RESPONSIBILITY
Employees and customers increasingly expect businesses to act responsibly. HR supports sustainability by embedding environmentally and socially conscious practices into company culture and employee initiatives.

What this says to me is that HR, as a function of organisations, is not going away, but instead there is an increased need for HR professionals to partner with organisations to deliver on their strategic people and culture needs. I'm not talking about the

administrative function of HR, I'm talking about HR professionals who are commercial and strategic, who understand the key
drivers of organisations and work with their client CEOs and
leadership teams to develop and implement strategies that drive
organisational results. HR is NOT about administration, the warm
and fluffy part of work, nor the police officer enforcer role – to do
our job well, we need to be a strategic business partner.

The HR function is a strategic partner driving business success.
By fostering cultures of inclusion, innovation and adaptability, HR
ensures organisations remain competitive, resilient and purpose-
driven in an ever-changing world. Moving into the future, this
function will be indispensable in aligning people strategies with
business goals and societal expectations.

For all these reasons, now is the perfect time to fly solo in your
HR professional career. As a self-employed HR consultant, you will
have the career standing that you deserve. Today's technology
enables you to build a sustainable business and deliver great
service to your clients. The increased complexities and reliance
around people and culture in business solidifies their need for
professional HR support.

CHAPTER 2

THE ALL-TOO-COMMON CHALLENGE: JUGGLING CAREER AND FAMILY RESPONSIBILITIES

Self-employment as an HR consultant can be the perfect occupation for a person looking to utilise their significant HR experience while balancing the needs of their family, ageing parents and personal ambitions. I say this because that's the life I'm living – and I've met many other bold, courageous people who have ventured into entrepreneurship for similar reasons. It can be tough, but I love it and don't regret my decision to start my own business for a second.

You'll see that I've focused this chapter on working parents BUT HR consulting is the perfect gig for any HR professional seeking flexibility in their lives – the professional sportsperson, the globe-trotter, the semi-retiree and those who are fed up working in the heartless (it's all about "shareholder return" or "people are our most important asset") corporate nine to five in a high-rise with a long commute and therefore no time to do what they are really passionate about. This book is for you too, and the time is perfect to take a leap of faith – in yourself.

I've interviewed many HR professionals over the years for consulting positions with Harrisons. Some of these women have tried working as solo HR consultants but struggled due to the challenges of self-employment – like the pressure of business development, fluctuating income and tax complexities. Many have shared that they miss the camaraderie of working in a team meeting the fundamental human needs of connection and belonging.

Currently, my entire team at Harrisons are women, mostly mothers. This wasn't intentional but rather the outcome of finding the best candidate for the job. Given the gender-skew of HR professionals (about 80% female) and women are the only ones giving birth, most of our applicants are mothers looking for flexible part-time. They seek part-time work, not just because their children need them but because they want to be present for those fleeting moments – school pickups, athletics carnivals, music recitals and even the ordinary family dinner. As mothers, we're often reminded: "They're only little for a short time." And it's true.

IT'S A GLOBAL MOVEMENT

Globally, women still face significant challenges in balancing careers with family. The International Labour Organization (ILO) reports that while 119 countries offer at least 14 weeks of paid maternity leave, others, like the United States, offer no national paid leave policy at all. Despite this, the burden of unpaid domestic work remains heavily skewed towards women. For example, in Greece, women spend over 4.5 hours daily on household chores, while men average only one hour. This invisible workload often limits women's career progression, reducing their ability to work full-time or pursue senior leadership roles.

This imbalance extends beyond the home. The global gender pay gap persists, with women earning approximately 20% less than men across all sectors. Even in the Australian public sector, women earn an average of 86 cents for every dollar men earn – a gap translating to $19,000 annually. When motherhood enters the equation, the gap widens. A University College London study found millennial mothers earn 16% less than men in the same roles, highlighting the long-term career impact.

The most recent Status of Women Report Card by the Australian Government showed that:

- 83% of one-parent families are single mothers
- women do over nine hours a week more unpaid work and care than men
- 43.3% of women work part-time versus 19.5% of men
- 35.7% of women cite caring for children as the main reason they are unavailable to start work or work more hours, compared to 7.3% of men
- 14% of employer-funded paid primary carers' leave is taken by men and 86% by women.

These realities paint a clear picture – women face systemic challenges in balancing their professional ambitions with personal responsibilities. This makes the choice to become an HR consultant even more empowering – because it offers the possibility of greater autonomy, flexibility and personal fulfilment while earning a good income.

TAKE A LEAP OF FAITH – IN YOU!

Starting your own HR consulting business can be a practical and fulfilling solution. You can design your schedule around your family, ensuring you're present for key milestones without sacrificing your professional growth. For some, this means working evenings or weekends to balance daytime family commitments. For others, it's about choosing not to travel frequently or avoiding long hours, which traditional roles often demand.

As a business owner and the mother of two teenagers, I've built a business model that allows me to experience precious family moments while staying connected to my clients and contributing meaningfully to my team. I still attend important business meetings, travel occasionally and participate in professional events – but on my terms. This sense of control over my career and personal life brings a deep sense of satisfaction, one I hope to help other women achieve. Thus, my author's intention for this book is **to help HR professionals transition from employees to business owners with work-life flexibility and financial stability.**

I've seen this balance play out in the lives of many incredible people I know personally:

- Donna, a single mother of a teenage daughter, pursuing her passion of leadership coaching after many years in HR roles of large organisations
- Kelly, a new mother seeking to balance her HR career while her husband's job requires frequent travel
- Allana, who plans to semi-retire soon, is working part-time to earn an income while travelling the world
- John, the grey nomad, who bought a caravan and travels the country with his wife while consulting
- Jodi, balancing ageing parents' care, a teenage son and a mortgage while leveraging her HR and psychology expertise for flexible income
- Chris, who has stepped out of his corporate role to work flexibly from home and enable him to spend more time with his young family while his partner steps back into her corporate career after taking time out for babies
- Ellissa, with three school-aged children and a husband who travels, thriving in HR consulting with the flexibility to be present for her family.

These people – and many others like them – are the inspiration behind this chapter. They are navigating the complex terrain of professional fulfilment, financial stability and personal responsibility, while pushing against global barriers.

ARE YOU INSPIRED TO TAKE THE LEAP?

This book aims to support HR professionals making the courageous choice to build a life on their terms. Whether you decide to run a full-scale HR consultancy or a smaller part-time practice, the framework I share will help you design a business that fits your life.

Using the IGNITE framework, you'll be guided to clarify your purpose – why are you doing this? Understanding your purpose is essential. If you aren't fully committed to the why, the inevitable challenges of business ownership will feel overwhelming.

IGNITE will also help you establish a structured business plan – because as the saying goes, prior planning prevents poor performance ("the 5Ps"). You'll be walked through defining your service offering, building your brand, managing your financials and exploring resourcing options. And most importantly, the framework will prepare you for the mindset shift needed to succeed as an entrepreneur.

But before we dive into the strategies and tools, I encourage you to reflect on what success means for you. For many people, success means achieving both professional growth and personal fulfilment without sacrificing family priorities. For others, it's about financial independence or simply having the flexibility to choose. Whatever your version of success is, this journey is yours to define.

Does self-employment as an HR consultant sound like the right option for you?

CHAPTER 3

IS HR CONSULTING YOUR CALLING? A REALITY CHECK

I love consulting and running my own business. It's something I always wanted to do. My plan was this – work in my corporate HR career until I turned 30, have babies and start working for myself. And that's what I did, except that I was 35 when I had my first baby. For me, I was chasing the accountability, challenge and ownership that comes with being a business owner – and the flexibility to work around the needs of my young family.

Knowing that I would be the recipient of the result of my efforts, good or bad, was (and is) a huge motivator for me. I was fed up with working huge weeks, travelling and stressing for the benefit of the corporate blood-sucking behemoth. Work, my career, has always been a significant part of my life, identity and passion. I was 110% committed to making it work.

READY TO STEP OUTSIDE YOUR COMFORT ZONE?
The most critical new skills I needed to learn were in sales and marketing. I have met many people who don't have an amazing amount of knowledge, skills and experience in their chosen business service or product, but they are successful because they are awesome at business development. This is a capability that I did not have to develop in my corporate HR role but it was a necessity to building my business.

Without clients there was no revenue, no business and no income for me and my family. So, I've learned to adjust my thinking around the dirty word of "sales", establish my personal and business brand, pick up the phone and not be scared of boldly putting myself out "there". "There" are all the opportunities to build my profile, establish my reputation and ultimately bring in leads to the business. "There" for me has included attending and presenting at networking events, partner events and our own events; expanding social media posting and connections; attending coffee catch-ups, business retreats and conferences – and all with perfect strangers! Each business owner has their own unique way of attracting leads and converting to sales but it is something that we all need to do.

TIME TO PUT ON YOUR BUSINESS HAT

Running an HR consulting business is not only about keeping your clients happy; there are many other ingredients that go into a successful business. I've talked about sales and marketing but other equally important areas are finance, resourcing and systems. Finance is about revenue but more importantly it's about profit. You need to be over your numbers, including your fees, quoting, margins, costs, invoicing, tax obligations and reporting.

Consideration also needs to be given about how best to resource your business to optimise client service and profitability. As a consulting business your major cost is people, and you are a heavily people-reliant business, which means you need efficient ways of planning and tracking time. This is something I learned early on from a mentor when I had a couple of employees. When we implemented a job costing and time tracking system, I became more considered about where I was spending my time once I could see where it was wasted. It's crude to say, but time is money in a service business.

Business ownership is not always easy, and it is not for everyone but for those who are suited to flying solo it is an amazing opportunity!

CHAPTER 4

EMBRACING THE FUTURE: HOW AI IS SHAPING HR CONSULTING

In my lifetime there has been an unprecedented rate of technological advancement that has significantly changed how we live and work. A few of you may remember the old dial-up internet connection? Goodbye fax machine! And then I was so incredibly excited to receive my company-issued Blackberry – most of you will need to search that! But hot on its tail came the iPod and then iPhone that revolutionised mobile communication forever. And then another exciting company issued tool – the laptop – I could work anywhere and anytime! There has been a proliferation of cloud-based systems, including HR, learning management systems, application tracking, time and attendance, and rostering. We've also experienced the rise and domination of social media platforms.

These technological advances have transformed the job of HR. For example, there are no more hard-copy personnel files – these have been replaced with automated application tracking systems. There's also the introduction of online employee communication platforms. Technological advancements such as robotics, automation and biotechnology have and will continue to majorly change work and life. But the most impactful technological change has arrived most recently, and that is the mainstream accessibility of generative AI – and it is transforming work.

AI is changing the shape of HR management, workplace culture, business and life. I see AI as an enormous opportunity to be an enabler of building your business and delivering consulting services. There are almost unlimited ways in which AI can be used to accelerate all areas of your business. However, based on my various experiences of using AI and technology at Harrisons, and with the disclaimer that it depends on the HR services you are delivering, clients remain committed to expecting a personal interaction with their HR consultant that is not AI delivered.

AI OPTIONS FOR YOUR BUSINESS
Now that I've said that, let's think about all the ways that AI can be used to help you in your new HR consulting business. AI is significantly helpful in content creation; everything from website structure and copy, articles and blogs, images, social media posts, scripts, presentations, and researching and drafting tenders. In delivery of client services, it accelerates the time you would normally need to meet client needs, such as drafting letters, writing position descriptions and reports, and analysing data.

It is critical that you understand and upskill yourself in using AI as an enabler for your HR consulting business. Due to the proliferation of AI products available with ranging features, benefits and costs, it may be overwhelming for you to decide what's best for your business. In this case, I suggest you talk to an expert about your options and what's best for your business.

BUYER BEWARE: AI CONSIDERATIONS
While AI presents an amazing amount of opportunities for HR consulting businesses, there are considerations before using it. Firstly, you need to make your own decision on how AI is used in your business and how that usage is disclosed to clients with reference to the laws and practices in your country and industry as specifically related to AI and privacy. Secondly, you need to carefully scope your needs, and then identify, review and select

the AI tools, systems and/or platforms that best suit your business as there is an ever-evolving range of AI options on the market. And finally, you need to develop your capability with AI as it is reliant on you providing the right information for it to be able to produce the best result for you and your clients.

AI, and other technological advancements, are the friends of HR consultants as they help us to focus on the value-add parts of our job that have the biggest impacts for clients and best meet our human need for contribution. While AI is saving us time on the "behind the scenes" work, it means we have more time to engage with our clients and team, connect with our professional networks, and contribute to our communities, families and friends.

CHAPTER 5

TOP 10 PITFALLS TO AVOID ON YOUR CONSULTING JOURNEY

Starting an HR consulting business is an exciting, rewarding and, at times, challenging venture. Along the way, there are numerous obstacles and pitfalls that can derail even the most promising businesses. However, by anticipating common challenges and avoiding the top pitfalls, you can build a consulting business that is resilient, profitable and fulfilling. Here, I'll share the top 10 pitfalls that new HR consultants often face, drawing on the insights and strategies covered throughout this book to help you steer clear of these challenges.

1. UNDERVALUING YOUR SERVICES

Many consultants struggle with setting their prices, often charging too little due to a lack of confidence or fear of losing clients. However, undervaluing your services not only impacts profitability but also diminishes the perceived value of your expertise. Remember, clients are paying for your years of experience, industry knowledge and the solutions you bring to their challenges. As discussed in *Chapter 23: Profitable Pricing: Value your Value*, make sure your pricing reflects the true value you provide. Always factor in your expertise, business costs and profit margin to ensure sustainable pricing.

2. NEGLECTING FINANCIAL MANAGEMENT

Poor financial management is one of the biggest reasons small businesses struggle. It's essential to keep a close eye on budgeting, cash flow and financial reporting from day one. Even if you're working with a bookkeeper or accountant, you must understand your financials to make informed decisions. In *Chapter 22: Essential Financial Practices for Consultants*, we cover the importance of establishing sound financial practices, including budgeting and cash flow forecasting, and setting aside funds for taxes and emergencies. Make financial management a non-negotiable discipline in your business to avoid unexpected shortfalls.

3. IGNORING YOUR NICHE

Trying to be everything to everyone is a common mistake among new consultants. Without a clearly defined niche, it's challenging to differentiate yourself, attract the right clients and develop targeted services. Identifying and focusing on a niche not only helps you position yourself in the market but also allows you to provide a deeper level of expertise and value to clients. Refer to *Chapter 12: Define your Toolkit: Your Unique Service Offering* and *Chapter 13: Stand out from the Crowd with your USP* for strategies on defining your niche and building services that meet your clients' specific needs.

4. FAILING TO DEVELOP A BRAND IDENTITY

A strong brand identity is crucial for standing out in a competitive consulting market. Without a clear brand, potential clients may struggle to understand who you are, what you stand for, and how you can help them. Developing a cohesive brand – including your business name, logo and messaging – helps clients connect with you on a deeper level and builds trust. In *Chapter 15: Create a Brand that Resonates and Sells*, we cover strategies for developing a brand identity that reflects your values and speaks to your ideal clients. Avoid this pitfall by investing time and effort into building a brand that makes a memorable impression.

5. RELYING SOLELY ON WORD-OF-MOUTH MARKETING

While referrals and word-of-mouth marketing are invaluable, relying solely on them can lead to an inconsistent pipeline of clients. A comprehensive marketing plan ensures a steady stream of leads and keeps your business top-of-mind for potential clients. As outlined in *Chapter 16: Your Essential Marketing Game Plan*, create a marketing strategy that combines content marketing, social media, networking and public relations. Consistency and multi-channel engagement are key to sustaining visibility and attracting new business.

6. SKIPPING THE SALES PROCESS

Many consultants feel uncomfortable with the idea of "selling" their services. However, without a structured sales process, converting leads into paying clients becomes much harder. Avoid this pitfall by mapping out a clear sales process that includes lead generation, nurturing and closing strategies. In *Chapter 17: Closing the Deal: Turning Leads into Paying Clients*, we discuss the importance of a sales process and shared steps for turning leads into loyal clients. Remember, sales is about building relationships and providing value, so approach it as an extension of your client service.

7. NOT SYSTEMISING AND SCALING

Failing to systemise your operations can lead to inefficiencies, wasted time and inconsistencies in service delivery. As your business grows, you'll need to implement systems that streamline processes and make it easier to deliver consistent value to clients. From project management tools to CRM systems and automation, technology can help you work smarter, not harder. In *Chapter 20: Work Smarter, not Harder with Tech*, we explore the importance of technology and systems in scaling your business. Ensure that you have a foundation of processes and tools that enable you to deliver high-quality service efficiently.

8. OVERLOOKING COST MANAGEMENT

Without cost control, it's easy for expenses to eat into profits, even in a profitable business. As your business grows, managing both fixed and variable expenses becomes increasingly important. *Chapter 24: Know your Numbers: Income and Exepenses* emphasises the importance of cost management for maintaining profitability. Track expenses regularly, budget for both predictable and variable costs, and avoid unnecessary spending. Remember, every dollar saved is a dollar that goes directly towards profitability.

9. BEING RELUCTANT TO OUTSOURCE

One of the biggest challenges for consultants is recognising when to outsource. Trying to do everything yourself can lead to burnout, inefficiencies and lower-quality work. Whether it's administrative tasks, bookkeeping or specialised services, outsourcing allows you to focus on your core strengths and strategic tasks. In *Chapter 18: Engage the Right Resources for your Business*, we discuss the importance of identifying the right resources, including employees, contractors and freelancers. Avoid this pitfall by focusing on tasks that drive value and letting experts handle the rest.

10. FAILING TO CONTINUOUSLY DEVELOP YOURSELF

In consulting, your knowledge and skills are your most valuable assets. Failing to stay updated on industry trends, tools and techniques can make your expertise outdated and less relevant to clients. Cultivating a growth mindset, as covered in *Chapter 6: It's all in your mind: Growth versus Fixed Mindset*, and investing in continuous learning will keep you at the forefront of your field. Attend workshops, participate in industry events and make a habit of learning something new every day. This commitment to growth not only benefits you but also adds value to the clients you serve.

CHECKLIST – AVOIDING PITFALLS IN YOUR CONSULTING JOURNEY

To help you stay on track and avoid these common pitfalls, here's a checklist you can use as a quick reference.

Set profitable prices
Ensure your fees reflect your expertise, experience and the value you provide. ☐

Practise financial discipline
Budget, monitor cash flow and manage costs to maintain financial stability. ☐

Define your niche
Know your target market, develop niche expertise and focus on serving those clients well. ☐

Build a strong brand
Invest in creating a cohesive brand identity that resonates with your ideal clients. ☐

Create a marketing strategy
Don't rely solely on referrals. Develop a marketing plan that attracts leads consistently. ☐

Follow a sales process
Develop a structured approach to lead generation, nurturing and closing. ☐

Systemise your operations
Implement tools and systems that streamline processes and improve efficiency. ☐

Manage costs proactively
Track expenses and prioritise spending that directly impacts profitability. ☐

Outsource where necessary
Focus on core strengths and delegate tasks that can be handled by experts. ☐

Commit to continuous growth
Stay updated, invest in professional development and embrace learning opportunities. ☐

Building a successful HR consulting business is a journey that involves hard work, strategic planning, and learning from both successes and setbacks. By being mindful of these common pitfalls, you can avoid many of the obstacles that derail new consulting businesses and stay focused on achieving your goals.

Remember, the pitfalls outlined here are not insurmountable. Every successful consultant has faced challenges and made mistakes along the way. The key is to learn from them, adapt and keep moving forward. By embracing best practices and maintaining a commitment to growth, you'll be well-prepared to navigate the complexities of consulting and build a business that thrives.

THE IGNITE FRAMEWORK

THE IGNITE FRAMEWORK

My **IGNITE** framework wasn't something I created in one sitting – it's the product of more than 15 years of experience building my HR consulting business, Harrisons, from the ground up. Along the way, I encountered countless hurdles and learned invaluable lessons, not just from my own journey but also from the incredible business owners across various industries whom I've had the pleasure of coaching, working with and learning from. These insights and experiences shaped what is now IGNITE: a structured, comprehensive guide to help you confidently navigate your own consulting business journey.

Starting out, I didn't have a clear pathway. Like many new consultants, I was overwhelmed, trying to balance client needs, market demands and the day-to-day of running a business, plus my young family. IGNITE emerged from this chaos as I developed systems to address each core part of the consulting business – from mindset and market understanding to branding and profitability. The goal? To create a framework that anyone could follow to bypass the initial growing pains and jump-start their own business.

IGNITE breaks down the essential stages into six key areas: **Inspire**, **Guide**, **Niche**, **Identity**, **Team** and **Earn**. Each of these stages solves a specific challenge. For example, in **Inspire**, we focus on building a resilient mindset – a foundation that helped me push through setbacks and stay motivated when I felt unsure. **Guide** teaches strategic planning, a skill I wish I had mastered sooner, as it transformed my business from reactionary to purposeful, allowing me to work toward long-term goals.

Each stage is designed to save you time, help you make decisions faster and avoid the pitfalls that often derail new consultants. In **Niche**, you'll learn to carve out your unique space in the market, focusing your services on the clients who need your expertise most. **Identity** dives into creating a brand that resonates with clients, a hard-won lesson from my own journey that showed me how vital branding is in attracting the right clientele. **Team** offers guidance on scaling, whether that means hiring, outsourcing or using technology to streamline operations. And **Earn** provides financial insights, teaching you how to price and manage expenses to keep your business profitable.

IGNITE is the blueprint I wish I had when I started. It's here to help you make sense of the unknown, feel confident in your decisions, and build a consulting business that reflects your strengths, serves your clients and grows sustainably. Through IGNITE, you'll have a clear, actionable pathway to build a business that not only fulfills your professional goals but makes a real impact in the world.

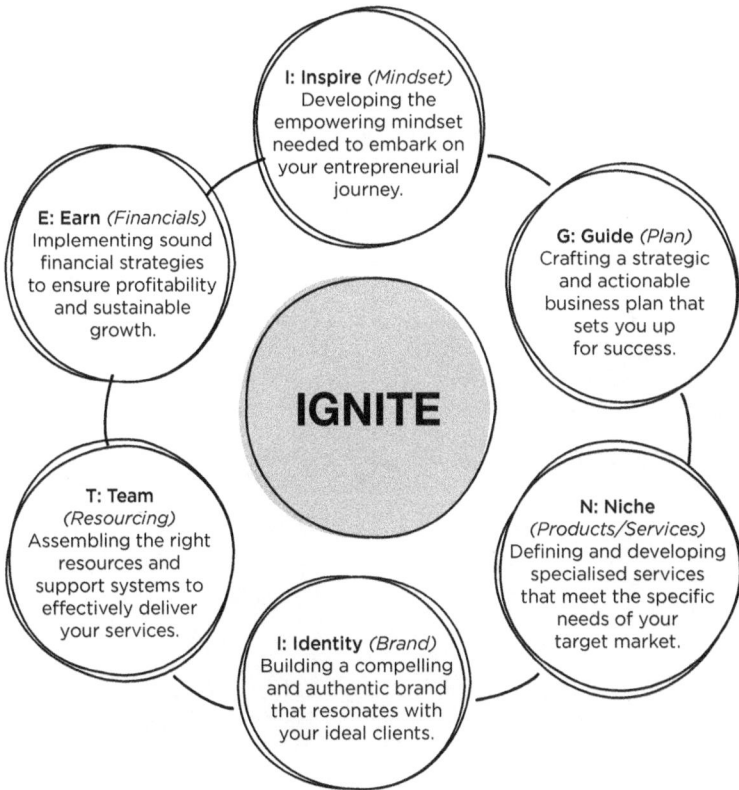

I: Inspire *(Mindset)*
Developing the empowering mindset needed to embark on your entrepreneurial journey.

E: Earn *(Financials)*
Implementing sound financial strategies to ensure profitability and sustainable growth.

G: Guide *(Plan)*
Crafting a strategic and actionable business plan that sets you up for success.

IGNITE

T: Team *(Resourcing)*
Assembling the right resources and support systems to effectively deliver your services.

N: Niche *(Products/Services)*
Defining and developing specialised services that meet the specific needs of your target market.

I: Identity *(Brand)*
Building a compelling and authentic brand that resonates with your ideal clients.

PART 1

INSPIRE

PART 1 – INSPIRE

When I first started Harrisons, I had no idea how much my mindset and habits would differentiate me for success. I assumed hard work and technical expertise were all I needed. But as I began to experience the highs and lows of entrepreneurship, I quickly learned that it's not just about what you know or how much effort you put in – it's about who you are, how you think and how you navigate the challenges that come your way.

Entrepreneurship is a wild ride. Some days, you feel on top of the world. Other days, you're questioning everything, from your decisions to your worth. Over time, I realised that thriving wasn't about avoiding the hard days and decisions but learning how to ride the waves. That's where the right mindset, daily habits and emotional intelligence come in.

Having a growth mindset is a game-changer. I had to stop seeing failures as personal defeats and start seeing them as lessons. This shift didn't come easily – it took years of practice, reflection and coaching. I began to notice how often I held myself back with thoughts like, *What if I'm not good enough?* or *What if this doesn't work?* Once I started replacing those thoughts with, *What can I learn from this?* and *What's my next best step?* everything began to shift. Progress became the goal, not perfection.

Daily habits also became my anchor. I'm not talking about rigid routines – I've never been a fan of overly structured schedules – but I learned the power of small, consistent actions. For me, it's things like setting intentions in the morning, carving out time to plan my week and prioritising self-care. These habits help me stay focused and resilient, even when things feel chaotic.

Then there's emotional intelligence – the ability to manage your own emotions and understand others. It's essential in this business. I've learned that how you respond under pressure defines your relationships, your reputation and ultimately, your success. For me, this meant practising self-awareness and learning how to handle stress without taking it out on those around me. It also meant surrounding myself with people who lift me up.

I can't stress enough how much your environment matters. Over the years, I've become more intentional about working with like-minded people – those who share my values of growth, integrity and positivity. It's amazing how much easier it is to succeed when you're surrounded by people who believe in you and inspire you.

I've also learned to recognise these attributes in others. When I meet someone with grit, curiosity and a knack for building meaningful relationships, I know they'll thrive in the long run. Those are the people I want on my team and in my network.

This section is about cultivating the mindset and habits that will sustain you through the entrepreneurial journey. It's not about being perfect; it's about being resilient, adaptable and open to learning. Because when you get the inner game right, everything else becomes possible.

Inspire is all about controlling the inner game that we all play in our minds that results in success or failure.

CHAPTER 6

IT'S ALL IN YOUR MIND: GROWTH VERSUS FIXED MINDSET

The trials and tribulations of starting a business can be daunting for some but invigorating for others! There will be setbacks, sometimes small and sometimes significant, but each time, your reaction to that setback is what will set you up for business success or failure. No matter how much time you invest in planning, there are always factors outside of your control. Sometimes they're within your control but you didn't do enough to mitigate the risk.

We are HR professionals, we work and are experts in the world of people, therefore we understand more than others the unpredictability of human beings. This unpredictability plays out in many and varied ways in your business; it could be a client who fails to follow your advice and ends up in court, or it could be an employee who decides to steal your client list and intellectual property and set up on their own. These moments will definitely test your resolve, which is why a growth mindset is imperative for every business owner.

TURNING SETBACKS INTO GROWTH OPPORTUNITIES

In the process of writing this book, my editor asked me whether there was ever a time I had to remind myself that a particular incident was a growth opportunity rather than a setback or problem. My answer? Every day. It's a constant practice of reframing challenges – not as failures or disappointments – but as opportunities to learn, adapt and improve.

One moment that stands out vividly happened not long before I was due to take a month off for a long-anticipated overseas holiday. It was a milestone celebration with family and friends – something I'd never done before – and I was incredibly excited. Everything seemed on track; I had a solid team in place and felt ready to step away. Then, out of nowhere, my Office Manager announced they were leaving.

The news hit like a ton of bricks. My plans for a smooth, well-earned break suddenly felt like they were unravelling. But instead of cancelling the trip, working myself to exhaustion or curling into a ball and crying (which was tempting!), I leaned into the challenge. I asked myself: *What can I learn from this? How can I turn this into an opportunity to improve the way we work?*

With that mindset, I set about creating a plan. I streamlined processes, identified tasks that didn't need to be done, implemented templates and systems, and hired a virtual assistant to support the team. The result? I only opened my laptop once during that month – and even that wasn't necessary. The experience taught me the power of planning, trust and delegation. Not only did I enjoy my holiday without a hitch, but I returned to a business that was running more efficiently than ever, with reduced resource requirements and greater clarity in our processes. Happy days indeed.

This experience reinforced a critical lesson for me: challenges are inevitable, but they don't have to derail you. Instead, they can be the spark for positive change, streamlining and growth. With the right mindset, even the toughest setbacks can become opportunities to make your business – and yourself – stronger.

ENTREPRENEUR CHARACTERISTICS

Some people are amazingly competent at the technical responsibilities of their jobs and/or highly intelligent, but this often doesn't correlate with the reasons for entrepreneurial success. Instead, I have observed that the most important characteristics and success predictors of entrepreneurs are whether they are:

- purposeful
- self-motivated
- inquisitive
- emotionally intelligent
- innovative
- strategic
- risk-tolerant
- problem-solvers
- resilient
- tenacious.

These are the successful entrepreneur competencies. Reflect on how you measure up against each of these competencies. As you reflect on the qualities of successful entrepreneurs, consider which ones you naturally embody and which may need development. If you uncover an area where you could grow, ask yourself: *How can I gain this skill?* Is it through reading, mentoring, training or simply stepping outside your comfort zone and practising?

And if you're unsure whether you possess these characteristics, don't worry – self-awareness is the first step. I dive deeper into this in the next chapter, where you'll find practical ways to assess your strengths, identify gaps and develop the mindset needed to thrive in business.

GROWTH MINDSET

The origins of growth mindset are in Dr Carol Dweck's work when she studied the behaviour of thousands of children. Dr Dweck coined the terms fixed mindset and growth mindset to describe the underlying beliefs people have about learning and intelligence. When students believe they can get smarter, they understand that effort makes them stronger. Therefore, they put in extra time and effort, and that leads to higher achievement.

Recent advances in neuroscience have shown us that the brain is far more malleable than we ever knew. Research on brain plasticity has shown how connectivity between neurons can change with experience. It turns out, if you believe your brain can grow, you behave differently. This began a series of interventions and studies that prove we can indeed change a person's mindset from fixed to growth, and when we do, it leads to increased motivation and achievement.

Neuroscientists have long understood that the brain can rewire itself in response to experience – a phenomenon known as neuroplasticity. Neuroscience shows embracing a growth mindset changes how your brain functions. Growth mindset is the belief that skills can be improved over time rather than being something we're born "good" or "bad" at. You may never be the best at something, but with a growth mindset, you know you can get better. Not only that, but a growth mindset also compels you to focus on improving – not proving – yourself to face all future challenges.

A Growth Mindset isn't just about believing you can improve – it's about actively seeking different perspectives to expand your thinking. One powerful technique I use in NLP coaching is Perceptual Positions. You may have heard the phrase "put yourself in someone else's shoes", but this method takes it a step further.

There are three key perspectives:

1. **First position** – Seeing the situation from your own point of view.
2. **Second position** – Stepping into the shoes of the other person, understanding their experience, emotions and motivations.
3. **Third position** – Observing the interaction from a neutral standpoint, as if you were an outsider watching without emotional attachment.

This third perspective is particularly valuable as it allows you to detach from the outcome, see patterns more objectively and make better decisions without the weight of personal biases. Entrepreneurs who master this skill gain greater emotional intelligence, problem-solving ability and resilience – key factors in navigating business challenges with clarity and confidence.

CHECKLIST – GROWTH MINDSET

So, what does that mean for you, as the founder of your HR consulting business? Here are my top tips for a growth mindset.

Take a breath
This might mean pausing before you respond to a difficult employee, sleeping on it overnight before you send a reply email to your arrogant client or taking three deep breaths before you go on stage to present at an industry conference to reduce the heightened emotion of the situation and best express yourself and remain calm.

Put yourself in their shoes
It makes a meaningful difference to think about how you would feel, think and respond if you were the other person, whether it be a client, employee or other key stakeholder. This will help you to find ways to improve your client and employee experiences.

Be strategic
Proceed with the end in mind. What is the desired outcome? Before going into any situation, whether it be a meeting, pitch or negotiation, be very clear on what the purpose of the meeting is and what you hope to achieve at the end. This helps to cut out all the peripheral discussion, data and alternatives, and instead stay focused on the end goal.

Gratitude
Every day find as many opportunities as possible to reflect on and acknowledge the positives in your life. At home, we do family dinners with gratitude – we ask each other what was the best thing about your day and why. At work, we do daily huddles covering your Win, Priority and Obstacle. Journalling, mindfulness and meditation are also excellent options for reflecting with gratitude.

Solicit feedback
Ask for feedback, especially from your current, past and future clients and employees. This feedback provides you with valuable insights to help develop yourself personally and also grow your business. This feedback may sometimes be difficult to hear but it is critical to you and your business.

Always learn
Continue to develop your HR skills, but now more importantly, your business skills to establish and grow your HR consulting business.

Positive peers
Surround yourself with successful business owners who you can learn from, contribute your ideas to their businesses, and as a bonus, build a network of referrers. These are people who will understand your challenges, provide you with encouragement to persist, and inspire you to stay focused on building your business. As per the concept, you are the average of the five people you spend the most time with.

Open-minded
None of this will work unless you are open to listening to other people, really listening and seriously considering what you're hearing. And then, taking the next step to implement these ideas into your business.

Innovation
Nothing ventured, nothing gained. Is there a new and better way of doing something in your life or business that could make a positive difference, big or small? If so, what's stopping you from giving it a try? It may not work but I'm confident you'll learn something from the attempt, especially if you take the time to sit back and reflect on the experience.

Curiosity
To be a thriving HR consultant and business owner, you always need to be curious. Curiosity helps you to innovate. Curiosity helps you to understand your clients' (real) needs and pain points. Curiosity helps you identify the motivations and desires of your team members. Be inquisitive, ask open-ended questions.

Remove "can't"
I was reminded by my gym instructor this morning that if you go in with the attitude of "I can't do this, it is too difficult" then you won't do it – I will never lift that heavier weight if I say I can't do it. Instead, at least, say that you are going to try, or even better, you are going to do it.

Own it
Ownership means taking full responsibility for your own progress, without excuses or blame. You can only control what you can control – yourself. How could I have done things differently? Work within what you can control. When reflecting on a current or past difficult situation, think about what your contribution is to the situation and what is the next best step you can take to achieve the desired outcome.

You do not have to be *the* most intelligent person to be a successful entrepreneur – or in most aspects of life. For my own professional and personal development, as well as business development, I have had the benefit of being part of several different entrepreneur groups and organisations. The people I have met in these groups range from start-up business owners right through to companies who have successfully scaled and sold, including publicly listing in a few cases. This has provided me with the opportunity to observe successful, and unsuccessful, entrepreneurs across a range of different industries.

In the next chapter I will talk about this psychology of success, specifically the inner game we all play.

CHAPTER 7

THE INNER GAME: MASTER THE PSYCHOLOGY OF SUCCESS

Like many things in life, to be successful in business, it mostly comes down to the inner game you're playing in your mind. Think of an ultra-elite sportsperson, such as Katie Ledecky, Michelle Payne, Simone Biles and Muhammad Ali, and how their mindset has taken them above and beyond the performance of others, overcoming obstacles to achieve their dreams over many years. These athletes teach us that greatness is largely psychological, and anyone can move closer to greatness by using the tools that have turned these athletes into legends.

Visualisation and self-talk can help you ditch self-doubt and channel the mindset of a champion. Many elite athletes mentally experience every single step of a competition the night before, from getting out of bed all the way up to accepting a gold medal at the awards ceremony.

Grit is a key ingredient in this secret sauce. Grit is the combination of passion and persistence that helps someone reach their long-term goals. Building more of it will make you more likely to achieve your goals.

INSPIRING WITH GRIT

Here are inspiring snapshots of remarkable individuals who have overcome tremendous challenges to achieve extraordinary accomplishments, each paired with a powerful quote:

- **Malala Yousafzai – Education activist**
  Shot in the face by the Taliban for advocating for girls' education in Pakistan, Malala not only survived but became a global advocate for girls' rights, winning the Nobel Peace Prize in 2014.
  "I raise my voice – not so I can shout but so that those without a voice can be heard."

- **Turia Pitt – Motivational speaker and athlete**
  After suffering burns to 65% of her body during an ultra-marathon, Turia Pitt defied the odds, becoming a motivational speaker, author and Ironman competitor.
  "You can choose your mindset, and you can choose your actions. You can choose to show up, no matter the obstacles."

- **Oprah Winfrey – Media mogul and philanthropist**
  Born into poverty and facing significant personal challenges, Oprah rose to become one of the most influential media personalities in the world, using her platform to inspire millions.
  "Turn your wounds into wisdom."

- **David Beckham – Athlete and philanthropist**
  After being publicly shamed for a critical mistake during the 1998 World Cup, Beckham faced intense criticism but persevered, becoming one of the most successful footballers and global icons.
  "The only time you run out of chances is when you stop taking them."

One of my favourite stories of grit is from **Diana Nyad**. In 2013, she did what no human in history had ever done before. The then 64-year-old swam unaided more than 100 miles from Cuba to Florida, spending over two full days in the water – without the safety and assistance of a shark cage. Soon after finishing the history-making swim, which Nyad had attempted five times before, she stood on the beach and spoke to the crowd that had gathered. "I have three messages: One is, we should never, ever give up," she said, "Two is, you are never too old to chase your dream. And three is, it looks like a solitary sport, but it takes a team." Diana's words reinforce three important factors in the psychology of success: persistence, belief and team.

EMOTIONAL INTELLIGENCE IN BUSINESS

To translate this to you and your start-up HR consulting business, we need to consider how you apply these practices in your life. A good starting point is assessing your own level of emotional intelligence (EI) as this will be a key component of helping to understand your "self". Emotional intelligence was a concept made mainstream by Daniel Goleman in the 1990s for personal use and at work. Emotional intelligence is the ability to be aware of and manage your emotions and the emotions of others.

People with a high degree of EI know what they're feeling, what their emotions mean and how these emotions can affect other people. My suggestion is to obtain feedback and data on your level of emotional intelligence. This can be achieved by asking for feedback on your EI from your current and/or past work colleagues who are comfortable providing you with honest and constructive feedback. You can also enter "free emotional intelligence survey" into your search engine and you'll be provided with numerous options to complete an assessment of your EI. This will help you to identify any gaps around your EI and implement a plan to develop these areas.

Without a high level of EI, it will be difficult to achieve success as a business owner. Having high emotional intelligence (EI) helps you as a business owner and HR consultant by allowing you to better understand and manage not only your own emotions but also those of your team and clients, leading to improved communication, stronger relationships, better decision-making, increased employee engagement, and ultimately, greater business success. Key aspects include empathy, active listening, conflict resolution and adapting to different situations based on emotional cues. This focus on EI will lay a platform for your psychology of success.

IMPOSTER SYNDROME

Imposter Syndrome is the persistent feeling that you're not good enough, you're not as competent as others perceive you to be, despite your experience, qualifications or achievements. It often shows up as self-doubt, fear of being exposed as a fraud or attributing success to luck rather than skill.

When starting your own HR consulting business, these thoughts can be especially loud. That nagging doubt – *Am I really qualified? What if I fail?* – can creep in, even for the most experienced professionals. But here's the truth: if you aren't feeling a little uncomfortable, you're probably not growing.

Rather than seeing Imposter Syndrome as a sign that you don't belong, reframe it as proof that you're stretching beyond your comfort zone. Every successful entrepreneur has faced moments of doubt, but what sets them apart is their willingness to push through. Self-belief isn't about never feeling uncertain – it's about trusting yourself enough to take action despite it.

Diana Nyad's incredible swim from Cuba to Florida wasn't achieved because she had zero doubts. It was because she refused to let them stop her. The same applies here – when those imposter feelings surface, remind yourself: *This discomfort means I'm evolving. I'm stepping into the next level of my career. And I belong here.*

NEVER GIVE UP!

Persistence and reliance are other key factors of your psychology for success. There will be setbacks and obstacles along the way, whether they be personal or business related. There will be hard days, decisions that don't go your way, an employee that resigns, a client who brings forward a deliverable date, a sick child – the list goes on . . . and on. You will be tested. You will need resilience, perseverance and tenacity to call upon to lift you up and keep going. Always keep an eye on the prize – your Big Hairy Audacious Goal (BHAG), your purpose or your "why" – whatever it is that resonates with you.

I've become very good, most of the time, at compartmentalising in these situations, especially when you need to keep moving to the next priority.

Some days, being a business owner feels like running a marathon before 9am. Mornings in my household are sometimes a whirlwind. My son, who has ADHD, used to, and occasionally still does, struggle with the rush, the routine, the organisation. Emotions run high, and getting out the door feels like an achievement in itself. This is easier than the early days of dressing and packing two toddlers for day care!

Then, it's onto the next challenge. I walk into the office, time to put on my happy, motivated, inspiring leader face. We kick off the day with a team huddle – energy up, focus clear. But then, the news lands. A tender I was optimistic about – one we'd poured hours into – has not gone our way. A setback, a gut punch, but no time to dwell. I take a deep breath and move on.

Next, a business development meeting. Stand in my Superwoman pose, and tell myself, "You've got this." It goes well and I secure the new client. After, a key employee drops a bombshell – they've booked a holiday at the same time as me. In a small business, that's not just an inconvenience; it means I'll be working on my holiday. I stay positive, adjust my mindset and figure out a plan.

Then it's home. Dinner, homework, life. Some days feel like an uphill battle. Others flow with ease. But through it all, I remain consistent in my thought – I love this. I love the challenge, the responsibility, the highs and even the lows. Because in business, as in life, you can't afford to dwell on the low moments. You reflect, you learn and you move forward.

Resilience isn't just about bouncing back; it's about pushing through, no matter what the day throws at you. You take a deep breath, stand tall, and tell yourself, "I've got this."

I'VE GOT THIS!
This leads me on to the next point made by Diana Nyad – **Belief**. Belief in yourself. Belief in the process. Belief that you will achieve your goal. You need to believe in yourself and back yourself. Sometimes, you may feel like an imposter – you don't feel up to the job, or think that others are better than you or that you don't have the right experience. We all feel that; completely normal.

But in those moments, you need to push through, sit with the uncomfortableness, prep yourself as best as possible, and put your best foot forward! We all make wild assumptions about other people; often assuming that others are better, more confident, more capable than we are when most of the time that is not the case.

BUILDING YOUR SUPPORT NETWORK: THE PEOPLE YOU NEED IN YOUR CORNER

As we've discussed, success in business isn't just about skill, strategy, or even hard work – it's about resilience, persistence and the ability to navigate self-doubt. The reality is, no entrepreneur builds a thriving business alone. Along the way, you will face moments of uncertainty, Imposter Syndrome, and challenges that test your self-belief. This is where having the right support network becomes invaluable.

We've already explored the importance of grit, persistence and mindset in the psychology of success. But even the most determined business owners need external support to push through tough times and stay focused on their vision. Here are the six key people and groups to have in your corner as you grow your HR consulting business:

1. BUSINESS COACH

A business coach helps you clarify your strategy, set goals, and stay accountable. When self-doubt creeps in or setbacks hit, they provide perspective and guidance to keep you moving forward. They ensure you're working on the business, not just in it, helping you stay aligned with your long-term vision.

2. PERFORMANCE AND MINDSET COACH

We've talked about Imposter Syndrome and the importance of self-belief – but overcoming these internal barriers isn't always easy to do alone. A mindset coach can help you reframe limiting beliefs, develop mental resilience and build the confidence needed to step fully into your role as a business leader.

3. YOUR EXISTING NETWORK

Surrounding yourself with the right people – mentors, peers and supportive colleagues – can make all the difference when your persistence is tested. Former colleagues, clients and industry peers can offer encouragement, share insights and provide valuable business opportunities.

4. ENTREPRENEUR ORGANISATIONS AND PEER GROUPS

There's power in learning from others who have been where you are. Groups like entrepreneur/business owner organisations, business chambers and industry networks offer mentorship, support and a sense of community. When business feels tough, being part of a like-minded group reinforces that you are not alone.

5. ADVISORY BOARD

As your business scales, having an informal or formal advisory board can help you navigate critical decisions and challenges. This might include experienced entrepreneurs, industry experts or financial and legal advisors who provide wisdom, perspective and accountability.

6. PROFESSIONAL ADVISORS – ACCOUNTANT AND LAWYER

Success isn't just about growth – it's also about building a sustainable and legally sound business. Having a trusted accountant and lawyer ensures you are financially structured for success, compliant with regulations and protected from risks that could derail your progress.

CHECKLIST – PSYCHOLOGY OF SUCCESS

Here are my suggestions to explore your psychology for success as a self-employed professional.

Find a coach

This will provide you with an objective sounding-board around your psychology of success. A good coach will support you in developing the mindset, emotional intelligence and resilience you need. A coach will also help you debrief those difficult situations for future learning application.

Create a vision board

Develop a visual image of your life goals that inspires and motivates you to stay the course with grit. A vision board is not just about your professional life, it's also holistic and needs to cover your personal vision for your life also.

Get clear on your BHAG

Set your Big Hairy Audacious Goal for your new business. Dream big. It needs to be a goal that motivates you to get up and go hard every morning. Then, make it very visible in your life by looking at it every day.

Visualise your ideal life

Create a very clear image in your mind of what that success looks like. Imagine yourself in that winning situation in your life. Run that in your mind over and over again so that it feels real. This is especially important for key moments of performance, such as a sales pitch or seminar presentation.

Self-talk is powerful

Filter out those negative belief thoughts that come into your mind. Instead fill your mind with positive thoughts and intentions, and say them out loud. Start each morning by staring at yourself in the mirror and telling yourself how fabulous you are and that today is going to be great!

Stand in your power pose
Ahead of a stressful or nerve-wracking situation, try standing in a high-power pose for two minutes. An example of this is the Wonder Woman, a pose that involves standing with your legs shoulder-width apart, chest out, with your arms placed on the waist. The effect? It can change hormone levels in the body by increasing testosterone (connected with dominance) and decreasing cortisol (connected with stress).

Develop your emotional intelligence
Complete your assessment and use it with your coach to identify priority areas to work on.

Live with grit
When things go off the rails, pick yourself up and keep going with a smile on your face!

The psychology of success is to possess and harness your ambition, grit and cadence. This takes a high level of perseverance on a consistent basis to understand your own emotional intelligence and inner talk, as well as being disciplined about that inner talk and your resulting actions. This topic of consistency and perseverance will be covered in the next chapter.

CHAPTER 8

PLAY YOUR LONG GAME, NOT YOUR SHORT GAME

Consistency, effort and perseverance are the ingredients of achieving long-term success. It all starts with the regular routine of tiny habits that you establish for yourself. Each tiny action takes you one step closer to your goal. Establishing that routine of daily, weekly and annual habits is so important in achieving the outcomes I desire. I'm not a military-style disciplined person nor prone to frequently setting life-altering goals, and too often I'm side-tracked by a new shiny object, but keeping myself structured around a routine of success habits ensures that I'm moving in the right direction.

THE SCIENCE BEHIND SUCCESS HABITS: DOPAMINE AND MOTIVATION

Developing success habits isn't just about discipline – it's about understanding how your brain works and using that knowledge to your advantage. One of the key drivers of habit formation is dopamine, the brain's "feel-good" neurotransmitter.

Dopamine is released when we anticipate and achieve something rewarding. This is why habits that bring instant gratification – like scrolling social media – are easy to form, while those with long-term benefits – like consistent networking or business planning – require more effort. The key to building sustainable success habits is harnessing dopamine to work for you.

Here's how:

- **Start small** – Your brain releases dopamine when you achieve small wins. Instead of setting overwhelming goals, break them down into bite-sized actions that you can celebrate along the way.

- **Create cues and rewards** – Pairing habits with immediate positive reinforcement (like ticking a checklist or treating yourself to a great coffee post-task) can help your brain associate effort with reward.

- **Focus on identity, not just outcomes** – Studies show that habits stick when they align with your identity. Instead of saying "I have to build my network," tell yourself, "I am someone who connects with others and builds strong relationships."

By understanding the role of dopamine, you can create habits that don't just rely on willpower, but actually feel good to maintain – paving the way for long-term success.

YOUR DAILY HABITS

What you choose to do each day, in each moment – your daily habits – will determine if you live the life you desire. This starts with your morning routine of getting yourself into the right mindset to make the most of your day. My day – and I am not a morning person – starts with:

- jumping out of bed when my alarm goes off
- splashing my face with cold water – and I like to brush my teeth straight away
- changing into the clothes I've laid out the night before, reducing the thinking required
- getting outside to soak up the sun's rays for Vitamin D, a serotonin boost, melatonin control and all its other health benefits
- moving my body, whether it's a silent walk, yoga or gym, even if only for 10 minutes
- setting my intention for the day and giving gratitude I'm alive!

Notice that I don't check or look at my phone as that would distract me. Plenty of time to check messages later.

That's my morning routine – yours might look a little different. If you don't have a regular routine, begin with one or two habits and build them up. If you may miss a day, that's okay, life happens. Pick it back up the next day, or better still make it up during your lunch break or evening.

PLANNING YOUR WEEK

When planning my work for the week, I always keep my overall goals and business plan in mind to ensure that every day I am doing something, even if it's just one small task, to bring me closer to my goal. For example, when writing this book, I chunked down the topics with a writing plan and word count, and each day I committed to writing 1,000 words. I find this thinking type of work best done early in the morning. For my first book, when my children were in primary school, I would wake up very early, go to a quiet space and write my 1,000 words very consistently. This time, I procrastinated a little but each day I did at least one small task that moved me forward on writing this book.

On a Sunday afternoon, I plan my and my family's week in a very full calendar with invites sent to my family and work colleagues as needed. I get clear on what needs to be achieved in the week. Then each day I identify the number one priority and ensure I allocate time to making it happen, around all the other multitude of professional and personal priorities. Everyone has a different way of tracking their priorities and you'll know what works best for you. I tend to use a physical journal for my priorities and tracking but electronic note-taking. With my team, I use online collaboration platforms. Before I finish work each day, and for the week, I look at what I set out to achieve and what needs to be carried forward.

RHYTHM OF WORK

With my team, I have a rhythm of communication. This rhythm includes daily stand-up huddles at the beginning of the day focused on wins, priorities and help/obstacles. We have scheduled weekly team and one-on-one short-sharp catch-ups, monthly values awards and celebrations, monthly leader meetings and quarterly team professional development and socialising, plus our annual conference. This rhythm keeps me on track. If it wasn't in place, it's all too easy not to schedule the meetings or get-togethers and they likely wouldn't happen. I prioritise these rhythms because they help me and the business stay focused on the right things.

This rhythm extends to our clients with monthly check-ins, monthly events, quarterly service reviews and annual awards. This structure and process needs to extend into the day-by-day service you provide to your clients. This means looking at your client journey and the key moments, and ensuring that you deliver on each of these critical milestones. Consistently delivering on these critical milestones strengthens client relationships and enhances your reputation. By exceeding expectations at every touchpoint, you not only add value but also cultivate Raving Fans who will naturally refer others to your business.

As I said earlier, your habits need to align to your goals. This will highly likely mean that you need to attract and win new clients. This cannot be done by waiting for them to come to you, or just setting up a website and posting on LinkedIn that you're open and ready for business. One of your most important disciplines will need to be picking up the phone and calling prospects. You need to be dogmatic in this discipline of engaging with potential clients. My advice is to make it part of your routine, set a target, and schedule a daily or weekly time slot to get it done.

Get obsessed with your processes. Elite athletes often rely on near-obsessive daily routines to keep their tasks lined up and their goals in sight. In everyday life, creating an effective "process" might be as simple as keeping a rigorous planner.

HABIT STACKING: MAKING PRODUCTIVITY EFFORTLESS

One of the simplest yet most effective ways to build consistency in your daily and weekly routines is through habit stacking. This technique, popularised by James Clear in *Atomic Habits*, involves pairing a new habit with an existing **one** – making it easier to remember and integrate into your routine.

The idea is simple: instead of relying on willpower to introduce new habits, you "stack" them onto things you already do. This helps create a seamless flow in your day, making positive habits automatic rather than an effort.

For example, if you want to start reviewing your business plan weekly, you could stack it onto an existing habit like your Monday morning coffee:

- After I make my first coffee on Monday morning, I will spend five minutes reviewing my top business goals and priorities for the week.

Or, if you want to make daily LinkedIn engagement part of your marketing routine, you could stack it onto something you already do:

- After I check my emails in the morning, I will spend 10 minutes commenting on industry posts and engaging with my network on LinkedIn.

By attaching new habits to established ones, you remove friction, making it far more likely that the habit will stick. Over time, these small, intentional actions compound, leading to greater efficiency, productivity and progress in your business – without feeling like extra effort.

CHECKLIST – SUCCESS HABITS

Use this checklist to build a sustainable routine that supports long-term success and personal growth.

Energising morning ritual
- Start your day with a positive, energising routine (e.g., stretching, journalling, meditation).
- Stack tiny habits to create momentum (e.g., drink water while journalling, stretch while reflecting).

Consistent, rewarding tasks
- Identify key tasks you can repeat regularly (daily, weekly, monthly).
- Set a schedule for these tasks to build rhythm and positive reinforcement.
- Acknowledge small wins to stay motivated.

Align your actions with your goals
- Break down long-term goals into short-term tasks and milestones.
- Review your action plan daily to stay on track.
- Adjust tasks as needed while keeping sight of the bigger goal.

Plan your week with intention
- Set aside time each week to plan key tasks and priorities.
- Ensure you schedule time for both business growth and client delivery.
- Use a mix of digital and physical tools to stay organised.

Use habit stacking for productivity
- Pair new habits with existing ones to make them easier to integrate. For example, review your business plan over your Monday morning coffee or make LinkedIn outreach a part of your email routine.

Create a rhythm for work and life
- Establish a structured routine for team check-ins, client follow-ups, and business development.
- Maintain a balance between consistency and flexibility to avoid burnout.

Prioritise your most important task daily
- Identify your most important task each day and allocate time to focus on it before distractions take over.
- Stay disciplined in moving key projects forward.

Stay focused on your 'Why'
- Reflect on your core purpose and values regularly.
- Keep your "why" visible (vision board, written statement or a mantra) to stay motivated, especially during challenging moments.

Practise self-compassion and flexibility
- Allow room for flexibility – progress, not perfection, is the goal.
- Release self-criticism when setbacks happen.
- Celebrate progress, no matter how small.

Build and maintain your support network

- Surround yourself with the right people – mentors, business coaches, accountability partners or entrepreneur groups. A strong support system keeps you on track and motivated.

Once developed, save your list of Success Habits as your screensaver and review it each morning to stay aligned with your goals and mindset. Consistency, not perfection, drives long-term success!

You don't have to be an elite athlete nor billionaire to appreciate and apply a routine of daily habits. No doubt a significant amount of consistent time and effort goes into establishing and building a consulting business. You will need to set goals and be disciplined about achieving them. This perseverance and determination will all be focused on achieving your personal and professional goals. In the next section of IGNITE, we look at Guide, which is about getting clear on your purpose and plan.

PART 2

GUIDE

PART 2 – GUIDE

When I first started Harrisons, I didn't fully grasp how critical it was to align my business with my intrinsic purpose. I knew I loved work – not just for the pay but for what it represents. Work fulfills some of our most basic human needs: connection, contribution, significance and growth. It brings people together, gives us a sense of purpose and challenges us to become better versions of ourselves. After becoming clear on my purpose, it has guided me in life: *to help people make meaningful connections and contributions at work.*

This purpose shapes everything we do at Harrisons. From the services we offer to the clients we serve, it's all about helping to create workplaces where people enjoy coming to work and are good at what they do. It's also why I'm writing this book – to help others build businesses that bring them and their clients joy. I've learned that when your business aligns with your personal values and purpose, it feels authentic. It's not just about making money; it's about making an impact.

But a clear purpose isn't enough on its own – you need a plan to bring it to life. Every year, I gather my team to create our business plan. We map out our goals and break them down into actionable steps. It's not just about setting targets; it's about getting laser-focused on what matters most. I also set personal goals every January for the same reason. Whether it's business or life, clarity gives you direction, and direction fuels progress. This process has been a game-changer for us, keeping our team aligned and ensuring we're always moving toward something meaningful.

Laying the groundwork for your consulting business starts here – with a purpose that inspires you, a clear understanding of who you're serving and a plan that connects the dots. It's about building a business that feels like an extension of who you are and what you stand for. When you get this right, the rest starts to fall into place.

Guide is about having a plan that guides and focuses your actions to your desired results – professionally and personally.

CHAPTER 9

DREAM BIG, PLAN SMART

Before embarking on your business ownership journey, it's essential to gain clarity about what you're striving to achieve. Why do you want to start a consulting business? What impact will this choice have on your life and the lives of those around you?

By taking the following steps, you can create a business that not only thrives financially but also reflects your purpose, values and desired lifestyle.

DEFINING YOUR IDEAL LIFE

Defining your ideal life means starting with the end in mind. This involves creating a clear picture of what a successful and fulfilling life looks like for you. Envision all areas of your life – career, family, health, personal growth, lifestyle and financial stability. This clarity serves as a compass, keeping you focused and motivated as you build your business. Consider these questions:

- What does an ideal day in your life look like?
- How much time will you spend working versus personal activities?
- What balance between professional success and personal satisfaction matters most?

USE IKIGAI TO IDENTIFY YOUR PURPOSE

A helpful framework for uncovering your purpose is the Japanese concept of Ikigai, which means "a reason for being". It involves the intersection of:

- what you love (your passions and interests)
- what you're good at (skills and expertise)
- what the world needs (market demand and impact)
- what you can be paid for (profitability and sustainability).

Exploring these elements can help you align your consulting business with your deeper purpose, ensuring it brings both financial success and personal fulfilment.

IDENTIFYING YOUR VALUES

Your values act as the foundation for your business decisions and relationships. Identifying them helps ensure you stay true to what matters most while building your business. Reflect on:

- What principles guide your personal and professional life?
- How do you want to be known by clients and colleagues?
- What values will shape your business culture and practices?

DEFINE YOUR PERSONAL LIFE GOALS – AND USE A VISION BOARD TO VISUALISE

Once you've clarified your values and purpose, it's time to set personal life goals. These goals should reflect what truly matters to you and keep you focused during your business journey.

A vision board can be a powerful tool for this process. It provides a visual representation of your goals and dreams, helping you stay inspired and aligned with your aspirations. To create your vision board, follow these steps:

1. Gather materials – use a physical board or a digital platform like Canva or Pinterest.
2. Select images and words – choose visuals and affirmations that represent your ideal life and business success.
3. Arrange with purpose – group visuals by theme – business goals, lifestyle dreams, personal growth.
4. Display prominently – keep it in a visible spot to reinforce your goals daily.
5. Review and update – adjust as your goals evolve.

APPLYING THESE INSIGHTS TO YOUR BUSINESS

Now that you have clarity on your ideal life, purpose and values, how can you apply these insights to the business you're building? Ask yourself:

- What type of business will best align with my ideal life and values?
- How will my services and client relationships reflect my values?
- What growth strategies will help me achieve both personal and business fulfilment?

My dream had always been to build a consulting business working with a team of fabulously talented and friendly consultants and having our own office space with an energetic and optimistic vibe. I wanted flexibility around my children, to be able to pick up from school and go to school events. Later, I also had a revenue target in mind that (for me) would mean I was a successful business owner.

However, another, and potentially easier option was to stay solo – consulting and working at home. This would have meant not having to worry about hiring and leading others, finding work for others, winning and satisfying more clients, and paying for office space and equipment. This brings extra complications. But, on the upside it means that I can go on holidays and the business keeps operating and producing revenue. It's also not as sensitive to the ups and downs of income as solo consulting – huge demand followed by no work because you didn't have time to secure new work.

BUSINESS VISION

After thinking about your purpose and what success looks like for you, you could further articulate your long-term vision by answering these questions:

- What is your business purpose/why? Why get out of bed in the morning? How will you make a difference to others' lives?
- What is your BHAG (Big Hairy Audacious Goal)? Dream big.
- What services will you provide?

- Who for? Who is your ideal client?
  - Industry?
  - Company size – revenue?
  - Company size – employees?
  - Client location?
- Where will you be based?
- What is your revenue target?
- How are you different from your competitors?

BUSINESS GOALS

Now that you've articulated the why and what of your vision, let's break down that long-term vision into actionable short-term goals for the first 12 months. To get started thinking around your short-term goals and actions, answer these questions:

- In one sentence, what is the reason the business exists? What do you do? What's the major outcome for clients?
- If the business was successful in the first 90 days, what would have been achieved?
- If the business was successful in 12 months, what would have been achieved?
- What are the five or six major areas of responsibility for you to focus on for the business to be a success?
- What are the tasks under each of these areas?
- For each area, how will you measure success?
- What are your business and personal values? Culture and behaviours for success?
- Financials – how much do you need to get started? What is your fee pricing model? Revenue by month? Budget costs by month? More on this is the Earn section.

CHECKLIST – YOUR IDEAL LIFE AND BUSINESS

Use this checklist to define your ideal life and develop a plan to make it a reality.

Clarify your ideal life
Visualise and document what success means for you in all areas – career, lifestyle, family and financial stability. ☐

Explore Ikigai
Identify the intersection of your passions, skills, impact and profitability to ensure your business aligns with your deeper purpose. ☐

Identify your core values
Define the principles that will guide your business decisions, relationships and culture. ☐

Set personal life goals
Establish clear and meaningful long-term personal objectives that balance work and lifestyle priorities. ☐

Create a vision board
Develop a visual representation of your life and business goals to keep yourself motivated and focused. ☐

Apply insights to business design
Ensure your business model supports your personal values, financial needs and lifestyle aspirations. ☐

Define short-term and long-term business goals
Set actionable targets for both personal fulfilment and financial success, breaking them down into 90-day and 12-month objectives. ☐

Outline your business vision
Clarify your purpose, ideal clients, services and long-term revenue goals to create a roadmap for sustainable success. ☐

Plan for financial viability
Determine your pricing model, revenue targets, start-up costs and financial goals to ensure business sustainability. ☐

Review and adjust regularly
Revisit your goals and vision at least annually to ensure alignment with your evolving personal and professional aspirations. ☐

Your starting point is to understand **why** you want to build a consulting business and what success truly looks like for you. Gaining clarity on your ideal life, core values and purpose will provide the foundation to stay committed and energised through your entrepreneurial journey.

By exploring your Ikigai, visualising success through a vision board, and setting both personal and business goals, you empower yourself to create a business that not only thrives but also reflects your unique vision and lifestyle. Let your purpose inspire every step forward, building a business that brings both personal fulfilment and professional success.

Now, let's refine your niche to ensure you stand out in the market.

CHAPTER 10

KNOW YOUR MARKET: CLIENTS, COMPETITORS AND REFERRERS

Market research is a critical step in developing your business plan. It is imperative that you identify your target market, understand their needs and analyse the competition. This will help you position your services effectively.

CLIENT AVATAR

A client avatar (also called an ideal client profile) is a detailed description of the type of client you want to attract in your HR consulting business. Think of it as creating a fictional but highly specific character who represents your dream client. This person isn't simply a vague idea like "small business owners" – they have a name, job title, industry, pain points, goals and buying habits.

Why is this important? Because knowing exactly who you're trying to reach makes your marketing efforts so much more effective. Imagine writing a social media post or email campaign. When you have a clear picture of *who* you're speaking to, your message becomes more focused, relatable and persuasive. A well-defined client avatar helps you:

- create targeted marketing messages that speak directly to their needs
- offer services tailored to their unique challenges

- save time and money by focusing on the right audience instead of trying to appeal to everyone.

To define your client avatar, start by asking yourself:
- Who do I want to work with? (For example: industry, business size, job roles)
- What are their biggest challenges? (For example: compliance, recruitment, employee retention)
- What goals are they trying to achieve? (For example: growing their team, reducing turnover)
- Where do they seek information? (For example: LinkedIn, industry events, HR publications)
- What drives their buying decisions? (For example: trust, expertise, proven results).

To further define your client avatar, visualise your perfect client is sitting in front of you. Ask yourself the following questions:
- Who are they?
- What are they saying?
- Why have they come to you?
- What are their problems?
- What is causing them pain?
- What keeps them up at night?
- What's their job?
- What's their company?
- How big is their company? Revenue? Number of employees?
- Industry?
- What is their demographic?
- Type of workforce?
- Where do they hang out?
- Who do they trust for business advice?

Draw or create a picture of them, give them a name, add all the above info and stick it on the wall in front of you. This is your client avatar. Get to know them very well. Think of this person every time you're developing your services, writing content or presenting a webinar.

RESEARCH YOUR CLIENTS

Now that you've established who your ideal client is, you need to undertake market research to really get to know them. Here are suggestions about how to do that:

- Get out of your office and talk to as many of them as possible. Where do they hang out? Go along to events, such as industry events, at those places.
- Connect and ask questions online.
- Join industry and professional associations, groups and forums online and in-person.
- Most people are flattered and helpful when you reach out to find out more about them, their business and industry. Schedule multiple coffee catch-ups each week.
- Run an online poll on social media on a topical and useful question for your market research.
- Facilitate a free webinar for your ideal target market, including a market research questionnaire.

KNOW YOUR COMPETITION

While I'm not a believer of worrying about the competition, it is important to understand who your competitors are, their value proposition, client acquisition and pricing strategy. This is an important area to cover when researching your ideal client as they are in a position to provide useful information. Suggested questions for your ideal client conversations around competitors include:

- Who are you currently using? How is that working for you?
- What do you like best about that company?
- What could they do better?
- How are their terms of service structured?
- What is the greatest value they provide?
- Have you used other companies? If so, who and why? Why are you no longer using them?

Internet searching is another great way to research your competitors, which you can do based on key words and locations. Look at their website and social media profiles. This will provide valuable information about their services, culture, brand and marketing strategies.

Another useful source of information is the referrers of services like yours. Who are they? Take the same approach with them as you did to research your clients. Connect with them, understand their needs and question them about your competitors.

CHECKLIST – UNDERSTANDING YOUR NICHE
This checklist will help you define your unique value proposition to attract your ideal clients.

Define your ideal client
Identify key attributes, including industry, business size, job roles and demographics.

Clarify client pain points
List their biggest challenges and frustrations that your services can solve.

Outline client goals
Understand what success looks like for them and how your services help them achieve it.

Identify information sources
Determine where your ideal clients seek advice, such as LinkedIn, industry groups, professional associations or word-of-mouth.

Understand buying decisions
Recognise the key factors influencing their choices, such as trust, expertise, pricing, referrals or proven results.

Research competitors
Identify direct and indirect competitors, their pricing structures, value propositions and client acquisition strategies.

Analyse competitor strengths and weaknesses
Understand what clients appreciate about competitors and where they may be falling short.

Identify key referrers and build relationships
Recognise who influences your target clients, such as accountants, business coaches and industry bodies, and establish referral partnerships.

Clarify your unique value proposition
Define how your services stand out, whether through expertise, approach, technology, pricing or level of service.

Test and validate your positioning
Use client conversations, networking, polls and marketing outreach to refine your messaging and ensure it resonates with your audience.

Now that you've clarified your vision, values, goals and niche – including your client avatar and competitive positioning – you're ready to develop your business plan for success.

Understanding your market isn't just a one-time exercise. As your business grows, industries evolve and client needs shift, regularly revisiting your client, competitor and referrer research will ensure you stay ahead.

The next step is bringing it all together in a strategic business plan that guides your decisions, actions and growth.

CHAPTER 11

IF YOU FAIL TO PLAN, YOU PLAN TO FAIL

Before you rush to announce your business to the world, let's talk about something absolutely fundamental: your business plan. This isn't just a fancy complicated document you create to impress potential investors or stakeholders. A solid business plan is your blueprint – your map for how you're going to get from today to success, however you define that.

I believe in keeping things simple and clear, which is why I'm a huge fan of a plan on a page. This approach not only helps you stay focused on the most important aspects of your business but also forces you to bring clarity to your goals, methods and success measures. It also works wonders for communication within your team, keeping everyone aligned and heading toward the same destination.

As the saying goes, "if you fail to plan, you plan to fail".

So, where do we start? Let's walk through the process together.

THE POWER OF A ONE-PAGE STRATEGIC PLAN

A traditional business plan can feel overwhelming, and let's face it, many of them sit gathering dust in a drawer. But a one-page business plan? It's short, sharp and gets straight to the point. More importantly, it's easy to refer to and use regularly. It helps keep your business agile, allowing you to make quick adjustments as needed while ensuring you're still on the right path.

Here's my one-page business plan template, which is designed for a 12-month period with quarterly focus areas.

Vision/ Purpose	This is your "why." Why does your business exist? What impact do you want to make? This isn't just fluffy motivational talk; your vision is what keeps you moving forward, especially on tough days.
Values	What core principles guide your culture and business decisions? For my HR firm, values like "Act with Integrity", "Back the Team" and "Delight the Client" are non-negotiable. They shape not only how we interact with clients but how we operate internally as a team.
Ambition (Three-Year Goal)	Yes, we're planning for the next 12 months, but you also need a sense of where you want to be in three years. This keeps you forward-thinking and stops you from only focusing on the immediate.
Theme	I love the idea of having a one-word focus for the year. This theme sets the tone for all your actions. For example, in my business, we've used themes like "Strive and Thrive," "Fired Up," and "Glow," depending on what we needed at the time. My team vote on the theme each year after the business plan is presented.
Capabilities	What does your business need to thrive? This could be anything from technology to a specific expertise.

Business Goals

Break down your goals into key categories:

Financial	Revenue and profit targets, but also think beyond that. How can you ensure you're operating a healthy business that's not only focused on growth but sustainable growth?
Brand	How will people see and experience your brand? Whether it's refining your brand message or developing your personal brand as the face of your business, it matters.

Client	How many clients do you want to serve? What kind of clients will help you build the business you want? This is also where I focus on quality over quantity, but you may decide to adopt a high-quantity, low-margin model.
Team	Your employees are part of your success. What structure and positions do you need to deliver on your plan? What are your employee engagement goals? How will you attract and retain talent?
Systems	This is the behind-the-scenes engine of your business. What systems need to be in place to streamline your operations? Think tech platforms, automation, AI and/or even more efficient processes.

Measures of Success	These are your indicators that you're on the right track. Examples include: <ul><li>profit/revenue/billables per consultant</li><li>client acquisition and feedback</li><li>Net Promoter Score (NPS)</li><li>employee engagement surveys and retention rates</li><li>system improvements and efficiencies.</li></ul>

Quarterly Focus Areas	Break down the year into quarters. This keeps you from feeling overwhelmed by a 12-month goal and allows for focus and flexibility. If something isn't working, you can tweak your plan each quarter.

Q1 – Focus Area	Q2 – Focus Area	Q3 – Focus Area	Q4 – Focus Area
3-5 key actions	3-5 key actions	3-5 key actions	3-5 key actions
Measures of success	Measures of success	Measures of success	Measures of success

PREPARING FOR YOUR PLAN

Before we kick off a new year of business planning, we spend time reviewing where we are and what's coming up. Here are the steps we follow to ensure the new plan is grounded in reality and not just wishful thinking:

- **Review performance against the current plan** – with my team, I take a hard look at what worked, what didn't and why. This isn't about blaming anyone or anything – it's about learning. What services brought in the most profit? What clients were most enjoyable to work with? What surprised you?

- **SWOT analysis** – a SWOT analysis is simple but incredibly effective. Strengths, Weaknesses, Opportunities and Threats. Be brutally honest here, because the insights will guide the next steps in your business. Do you have strengths that aren't being fully leveraged? Are there market trends or opportunities that you can capitalise on?

- **Client survey or interviews** – don't assume you know what your clients think – ask them! We regularly conduct client surveys or one-on-one interviews to get feedback. You might think a service is invaluable, but if your clients aren't using it or don't find it helpful, it's time to reevaluate.

- **Market competitor research** – keep an eye on what's happening in your industry. What are your competitors doing well, and what can you learn from them? But also, where are they lacking? There could be gaps in the market that you're perfectly positioned to fill.

- **Financial analysis** – review your financials closely. Which services are most profitable? What's your average invoice size, and is it growing? Who are your most valuable clients, and how can you find more like them?

OVERCOMING MINDSET BLOCKS IN BUSINESS PLANNING

Business planning isn't just about strategy and numbers – it's also a powerful exercise in self-awareness. As you map out your vision, goals and action steps, take a moment to notice what thoughts and feelings come up. Do you feel excited and motivated, or do you experience hesitation, uncertainty or self-doubt? Sometimes, negative self-talk or a sense of overwhelm can creep in – these may be mindset blocks that could limit your progress.

If you find yourself thinking "I don't know if I can do this" or "What if I fail?", recognise that these thoughts are natural but not necessarily true. Addressing these blocks is just as important as refining your plan. Revisit the **Inspire** section, where we explore the role of mindset in business success. And if these doubts persist, consider working with a mindset coach or using strategies like reframing, journalling or perceptual positions (covered in the Growth Mindset section) to shift your perspective. Your plan is only as strong as your belief in yourself to execute it.

IMPLEMENTING THE PLAN

Once you've reviewed your current year, conducted research and crafted your new plan, it's time for implementation. Here's how to ensure your plan isn't just a document that sits in a drawer:

- **Communicate** – make sure everyone on your team understands the plan. It's one thing to write down goals, but they won't get done unless people are aware and aligned with them.
- **Review regularly** – don't wait until the end of the year to see how you're tracking. Review your plan quarterly, at a minimum. Adjust and pivot as necessary but stay focused on the overall goals.
- **Celebrate wins** – when you hit milestones, take the time to acknowledge and celebrate them. This builds momentum and keeps your team motivated.

CHECKLIST – CREATING AND IMPLEMENTING YOUR BUSINESS PLAN

Use this checklist to create a clear, actionable business plan that aligns with your vision, keeps you focused and drives sustainable growth.

Clarify your vision and purpose
Define why your business exists, the impact you want to make and how your business aligns with your long-term goals. ☐

Identify your core values
Establish the principles that will guide your decisions, shape your company culture, and influence client and team interactions. ☐

Set your three-year ambition
Look beyond the next 12 months and articulate where you want your business to be in three years to ensure long-term focus. ☐

Choose your annual theme
Select a one-word theme or phrase that sets the tone for the year and keeps your team aligned with a shared focus. ☐

Define key business goals
Break down financial, brand, client, team and systems goals to ensure a well-rounded strategy for sustainable growth. ☐

Establish measurable success indicators
Determine how you'll track progress, such as revenue targets, client satisfaction scores, employee engagement metrics or operational efficiencies. ☐

Plan quarterly focus areas
Divide the year into four quarters and assign specific focus areas with 3-5 key actions for each to maintain momentum and adaptability. ☐

Conduct a business review before planning
Evaluate your past performance, conduct a SWOT analysis, gather client feedback, research competitors and assess financial data to make informed decisions. ☐

Address mindset blocks
Recognise and overcome self-doubt, limiting beliefs or hesitation by revisiting the mindset principles outlined in the INSPIRE section.

Implement, communicate and review regularly
Ensure your plan is a living document by sharing it with your team, revisiting it quarterly and making necessary adjustments to stay on track.

In short, your business plan is more than just a roadmap – it's a living document that should evolve as your business grows. By keeping it simple, clear and actionable, you're setting yourself up for success. Remember, the goal isn't to make everything perfect but to take consistent, meaningful steps toward your vision.

Now it's time to put your plan into action. Download the **one-page business plan template** using the link at the end of the book and start crafting your blueprint for success.

PART 3

NICHE

PART 3 – NICHE

I'll never forget the moment I realised I was trying to be everything to everyone in my consulting business. In those early years, I said yes to any client request, no matter how far outside my expertise it was. I thought flexibility and customisation was the key to success, but instead, it left me overwhelmed and stretched too thin – both with time and money. Clients were confused about what I actually offered, and honestly, so was I. It wasn't until about five years in that I discovered the power of niching down and building services that were not only clear but also repeatable and scalable.

One of my biggest lessons was the importance of creating an entry-level product that introduced clients to what we do. I realised that people don't automatically jump into your highest-value services – they need to trust you first. Developing these smaller, accessible products not only built that trust but also allowed me to focus on the core services that truly made an impact. This shift helped us stand out in the market, made our offerings easier to explain and sell, and brought consistency to our revenue.

When I first launched Harrisons, I believed our core retainer product – a premium, long-term service – would be an instant hit. But I quickly learned that clients weren't ready to commit to such a significant investment without first understanding how we worked. By offering smaller, entry-point services like HR health checks or strategy sessions, clients were able to experience our expertise, build trust and see our value. Many of those clients later transitioned to our core retainer product, proving that sometimes starting small is the key to building big, lasting relationships.

Another game-changer was learning to design services with my clients' needs in mind – not only what I thought they needed. It sounds obvious, but I can't tell you how many times I created offerings based on my assumptions rather than what clients actually wanted. Asking the right questions and listening closely transformed how we worked.

Today, many of our services are based on monthly recurring income, which is a win-win for both us and our clients. It brings stability to our business and allows clients to count on ongoing support. This section is all about helping you take your expertise, define it clearly, and turn it into a sustainable, profitable business model. Trust me – when you get this right, everything changes.

Niche is about identifying and defining your product for a profitable business model.

CHAPTER 12

DEFINE YOUR TOOLKIT: YOUR UNIQUE SERVICE OFFERING

One of the most important steps in starting your HR consulting business is getting crystal clear on what's in your toolkit – what products and services you're going to offer. It's easy to fall into the trap of thinking that offering a wide range of services will attract more clients. But here's the reality: clarity is key. The more focused and defined your service offerings are, the more efficiently and profitably you'll be able to run your business.

When you clearly define your services, it becomes easier to communicate with clients, align your marketing and build a reputation for expertise. Rather than trying to be a jack-of-all-trades, you're positioning yourself as a specialist in a few key areas, which allows you to deliver greater value, be more profitable and scale your business more effectively.

Defining your services isn't a one-time exercise – your business will evolve, and so should your offerings. That's why it's essential to revisit and refine your service toolkit annually, ensuring it aligns with market trends, client needs and your business goals.

MY STORY: THE CHALLENGES OF CUSTOMISATION

When I first started Harrisons, I made the same mistake as many new consultants – I offered everything to everyone. I didn't have a clear service offering, and I wanted to cater to every client's unique needs. It seemed like the right approach at the time. I was a solo consultant and figured that the more flexible I could be, the more attractive I'd be to potential clients. I'd customise my services entirely, building bespoke solutions for each client, tailoring everything to their specific challenges.

At first, this approach felt rewarding. Clients loved that they were getting personalised, hands-on service, and I enjoyed the challenge of creating something unique for each of them. But soon enough, the cracks began to show, and I realised I was building a business that wasn't sustainable.

I felt like I was running on a treadmill – constantly working, but not getting anywhere. I vividly remember one particularly hectic period where I was juggling several custom projects simultaneously. I was pulling late nights, skipping meals and putting off any form of rest or downtime. But the worst part? I was missing out on quality time with my young children. I'd be physically present, but my mind was always racing – worrying about the next client, the next deadline or the next customised solution I had to create. The realisation hit me hard: I had built a business that was supposed to give me more flexibility, yet it was consuming every part of my life.

Burnout hit me hard. It wasn't just physical exhaustion; it was mental and emotional, too. I became irritable, overwhelmed and started resenting the very work I once loved. My relationships suffered, and I wasn't the present, engaged parent I wanted to be. I remember breaking down to a coach I was working with at the time, venting about how I couldn't keep up with the demands of customising every service. Their advice was invaluable: "Your time is your most valuable asset. If you keep selling it in a way that drains you, you won't have a business, and you won't have a life." That was my epiphany moment.

Making those changes wasn't easy. Systemising and productising my services required me to take a hard look at my business and let go of the belief that every client needed a completely unique solution. I started by identifying the common threads across my projects – the services I was delivering repeatedly and the challenges most clients faced. From there, I built structured service packages that could address these common needs efficiently and effectively.

I won't sugarcoat it – letting go of the "everything to everyone" approach was hard. I worried I'd lose clients who wanted customisation. But what I discovered was the opposite: having clear, structured offerings made it easier for clients to understand what I did and the value I brought. It freed up my time, reduced my stress and allowed me to finally take holidays without my laptop glued to my side. Most importantly, it gave me back quality time with my family.

The shift to systemising and productising my services was a game-changer. I built a business that didn't rely solely on me, improved profitability, and created space for growth and scalability. It wasn't an overnight fix, but it was worth every ounce of effort. Now, I want to help you make that same transformation – one that leads to freedom, sustainability and a business you love.

YOUR UNIQUE SERVICE OFFERING: THE THREE-STEP PROCESS

Building a successful HR consulting business isn't just about doing the work – it's about doing the right work. The key to a scalable and profitable business is developing services that align with both your expertise and what the market truly needs. Without a clear, structured service offering, you risk spreading yourself too thin, over-customising solutions and limiting your ability to grow.

The three steps below will help you create a service offering that is fulfilling, profitable and scalable. First, you'll define what you love doing and where your expertise lies. Second, you'll assess whether there's real demand and profitability for these services. Finally, you'll systemise your delivery so that you can scale effectively while maintaining quality.

By following this process, you'll develop a service offering that not only brings value to clients but also creates a business that works for you – not one that runs you into the ground. Let's break it down.

STEP 1: SELECTING THE RIGHT SERVICES
The first step in defining your services is figuring out what you love to do and what you're great at delivering. What lights you up? What gets you out of bed in the morning? These are the services that will keep you motivated and inspired. But passion alone isn't enough – you also need to consider what your clients actually need.

Ask yourself: What problems are my clients facing that I can solve? This is the sweet spot where your passion intersects with market demand, as we covered earlier with Ikigai. It's here that you'll find the services that are not only fulfilling to you but also valuable to your clients. For example, in my business, we quickly realised that core services like HR strategy, compliance and leadership training were in high demand. Focusing on these aspects allowed us to deliver maximum impact while staying true to what we enjoyed and excelled at.

STEP 2: REALITY CHECK – MARKET INTEREST AND PROFITABILITY
Once you've identified the services you want to offer, it's time for a reality check. No matter how much you love offering a particular service, if no-one is willing to pay for it, you won't get very far.

Research the market. Are there other businesses offering similar services? What are their price points? Most importantly, is there enough demand to make your service offering viable? If you're passionate about a particular service but find that it isn't profitable or that the market is oversaturated, it might be time to tweak your approach.

For me, one of the most valuable lessons was understanding that not every service idea is a winner. Sometimes the market simply isn't there, and that's okay. It's better to pivot early than to pour resources into something that won't pay off in the long run. The goal here is to find services that are not only fulfilling but also profitable and scalable.

STEP 3: SYSTEMISING YOUR SERVICES

Once you've refined your service offerings and confirmed their viability, the next step is systemising them. Systemisation is about creating processes that ensure consistency, efficiency and scalability. This doesn't mean stripping away the personal touch; it means building a foundation that allows you to consistently deliver high-quality services without burning yourself out.

If you're just starting out, you may not have access to state-of-the-art systems – and that's okay. Systemising doesn't mean expensive software or complex automation; it starts with simple, repeatable processes. Even as a solo consultant, small efficiencies like checklists, templates and structured workflows can save you hours of time and prevent costly mistakes. I've wasted valuable time in the past due to a lack of systemisation, and I've seen many start-ups struggle because they're constantly reinventing the wheel. The key is to put just enough structure in place to ensure consistency and prevent overwhelm, without overcomplicating things.

Here are a few things that worked for me:

- **Document everything** – every step involved in delivering a service needs to be documented. This includes timelines, resources, tools and specific processes. When everything is documented, it becomes easier to onboard new team members and maintain quality control as your business grows.
- **Create templates** – wherever possible, develop templates for proposals, client onboarding and service delivery. This will save time and ensure that nothing gets overlooked.
- **Use technology to automate** – leverage technology to streamline repetitive tasks like scheduling, invoicing and follow-ups. This frees you up to focus on higher-value activities, like client relationships and strategic growth.

Whether you're a solo consultant or leading a team, systemising your services will help you work smarter, not harder. It ensures consistency, saves time, and allows you to scale your business without losing control of quality. Most importantly, it helps you focus on growing your business, rather than constantly being caught up in day-to-day delivery.

CHECKLIST – SYSTEMISING SERVICES

Here's a quick checklist to keep you on track as you define and systemise your services.

Define your core services with clarity
Write down the specific HR services you will offer, ensuring they align with your expertise and client needs (for example, HR strategy, compliance audits, leadership training).

Identify scalable service models
Review your offerings and determine if they can be delivered repeatedly without relying solely on your personal involvement. Adjust services to reduce reliance on customisation.

Validate market demand
Research your ideal clients' pain points and confirm there is sufficient demand for your services. Speak with potential clients, review competitors and assess industry trends.

Ensure profitability and sustainability
Calculate the time, resources and costs associated with each service. Set pricing that reflects your value while ensuring profitability and long-term sustainability.

Document your service delivery process
Outline every step of delivering each service, from initial client contact to project completion. Include tools, timelines and quality checkpoints to standardise your approach.

Create and use templates
Develop standard templates for proposals, client agreements, onboarding processes and service reports to save time and ensure consistency in client communication.

Implement technology for efficiency
Adopt software tools like scheduling platforms, CRMs and project management systems to automate repetitive tasks and streamline service delivery.

Train and empower your team
Document processes so clearly that a team member or contractor could deliver your services without your direct involvement. Provide training and access to resources for consistency.

Test and refine your service model
Pilot your service packages with a small client group and gather feedback. Use insights to refine your processes, pricing and templates before scaling further.

Review and optimise regularly
Schedule regular check-ins to assess service performance, client feedback and profitability. Adjust as needed to stay competitive and maintain quality service delivery.

If you follow this checklist of actions, you'll create a structured, efficient and scalable consulting business that allows you to grow, stay profitable and maintain work-life balance. By getting clear on your service offerings and systemising them for maximum impact, you'll set yourself up for success. You'll not only be able to grow and scale your business but also have the freedom to step back when needed – without everything falling apart. And trust me, that's a game-changer.

Next, we'll look at how you stand out from the crowd in comparison to your competitors.

CHAPTER 13

STAND OUT FROM THE CROWD WITH YOUR USP

In the crowded world of HR consulting, standing out can feel like a daunting challenge. Many businesses offer similar services, there are huge players in the market and potential clients can easily be overwhelmed by the options. This is where your **Unique Selling Proposition (USP)** – or value proposition – comes into play. A compelling value proposition clearly communicates why someone should choose your company and services over others. It's not just about what you do, but how you do it differently and why that matters. Ultimately, the purpose of a strong USP is to attract and retain clients, ensuring the long-term success of your business.

When you're starting an HR consulting firm, defining your value proposition from the outset is crucial. It helps potential clients understand the unique value you bring to the table and sets the tone for all your marketing and business development efforts. Your USP should act as a magnet, drawing in clients who resonate with your approach and values while setting you apart from the competition.

WHAT IS A USP AND WHY IS IT IMPORTANT?
A USP, or unique selling proposition, is a clear statement that defines what makes your business different from everyone else.

In simpler terms, it's the answer to the question, "Why should a client choose you over someone else?"

For a start-up HR consulting business, your USP is particularly important because it helps you establish your brand in a competitive market. You're not just another HR consultant offering generic services; you're positioning yourself as the go-to expert for a specific problem, niche or type of client. Your USP helps communicate your expertise, build trust with potential clients and foster loyalty with existing ones.

The goal of a USP is twofold: attraction and retention. It should immediately catch the attention of potential clients by highlighting the benefits and unique aspects of your services. At the same time, it should foster long-term relationships, keeping clients engaged and coming back for more.

HOW HARRISONS CREATED ITS USP

At Harrisons, creating our USP has been central to our success. When I started out, I didn't have a clearly defined value proposition. Like many new consultants, I was focused on delivering quality work but hadn't yet homed in on what made my business special. Over time, I realised that I needed to differentiate myself, especially as the competition grew.

For us, the key was understanding who we were serving and what they really needed. We refined our focus to working with small and medium-sized enterprises (SMEs). These businesses often lacked the resources or expertise to manage complex HR issues in-house but couldn't afford large-scale consulting firms. That's where we came in.

Our USP became, "Your personalised HR team, dedicated to business success and growth". This clearly communicated that we aren't just an outsourced service; we are a strategic partner who cares about our clients' success. By framing ourselves as their HR team, we position Harrisons as an extension of their business rather than just another external consultant. This approach creates a sense of trust and collaboration, which helps us stand out in a crowded marketplace.

This value proposition has worked wonders for us. It's been instrumental in attracting warm leads and referrals, which, as any business owner knows, are the lifeblood of sustainable growth. Word-of-mouth referrals, driven by a clear and compelling USP, have been critical in growing the business year after year.

STEPS TO CREATING YOUR USP

Now that you understand what a USP is and why it's important, let's walk through the three steps to create your own compelling value proposition.

1. DEFINE WHAT YOU DO DIFFERENTLY

Start by identifying the unique aspects of your service offering. What sets you apart from others in the HR consulting space? This doesn't have to be something earth-shattering, but it does need to be something that resonates with your target market – and you.

Maybe you have deep expertise in a particular industry, or you're known for your hands-on approach. Perhaps you're an expert in navigating workplace compliance for SMEs, or your firm offers a specific HR software solution that streamlines processes for your clients. Whatever it is, make sure it's something that truly differentiates you from your competitors and provides a clear benefit to your clients.

Ask yourself:

- What am I especially good at?
- What pain points do my services solve for my clients?
- How do my services improve my clients' lives or businesses?

In the case of Harrisons, our key differentiator is that we positioned ourselves as **partners in business growth**, not just problem-solvers. We help clients with their HR strategy in a way that aligns directly with their business goals.

2. UNDERSTAND HOW YOU'RE DIFFERENT FROM COMPETITORS

To develop a compelling USP, you need to know who your competitors are and what they offer. This will allow you to identify gaps in the market where your services can shine. Competitor analysis doesn't have to be complicated. Start by looking at the websites of other HR consultants in your niche, paying close attention to how they position their services.

Once you have a clear understanding of your competitors, ask yourself:

- How is my service offering different from theirs?
- What can I do better or more efficiently?
- What pain points do clients have with competitors that I can address?

The goal here is to identify the "white space" – the area where your services can fill a need that isn't being met by others. For Harrisons, this white space was the fact that many SMEs didn't have access to personalised, strategic HR support tailored to their specific growth goals rather than just reactive compliance advice.

3. COMMUNICATE YOUR USP CLEARLY AND EFFECTIVELY

Once you've defined your unique value proposition and analysed how it differentiates you from competitors, the next step is communicating it effectively. A great USP is only valuable if your target audience understands it.

This is where your marketing and communication strategy comes into play. Make sure your USP is front and centre on your website, in your pitch to clients and throughout your marketing materials. Your messaging should consistently reflect your value proposition.

For example, Harrisons communicates our value proposition through language that highlights our personalised, partner-based approach to HR. Whether it's on our website, in our social media posts or during initial client meetings, we make it clear that we're more than just an external consultant – we're part of their team.

In the next section of IGNITE – **Identity** – we'll go deeper into how to communicate your brand and value proposition, but for now, ensure that your USP is prominent and easily understood by your clients. Remember, clarity is key.

CHECKLIST – CREATING YOUR USP

Now that you understand what a USP is and why it's important, let's walk through the steps to create your own compelling value proposition.

Define what you do differently
Ask yourself:
- What am I especially good at?
- What pain points do my services solve for my clients?
- How do my services improve my clients' lives or businesses?

Understand how you're different from competitors
Start by looking at the websites of other HR consultants in your niche, paying close attention to how they position their services.

Identify your ideal client
Clarify your ideal client profile, including their needs, challenges and goals. Tailor your USP to resonate with this audience.

Focus on client outcomes and benefits
Your USP should highlight how you create value for your clients. Focus on tangible outcomes.

Use clear and simple language
Avoid jargon or complex statements. If you can't explain it in one or two sentences, simplify it further.

Validate with feedback
Ask for feedback from a few trusted clients to ensure it resonates and clearly differentiates your services.

Integrate your USP into your marketing
Once defined, ensure your USP is visible on your website, social media, business cards and proposals.

Train your team on your USP
If you have a team, ensure they understand and can communicate your USP consistently.

Evolve your USP over time
As your business grows, revisit and refine your USP. Client needs, market trends and your services may evolve.

Measure the impact of your USP
Track how your USP affects lead generation, client retention and referrals. If it's not attracting the right clients, consider refining it.

By following these steps and crafting a value proposition that resonates with your target clients, you'll position your business to stand out in the crowded HR consulting space. A strong USP doesn't just attract clients – it builds loyalty, fosters referrals and ensures long-term business success.

Once you attract these ideal clients, it's important to ensure your services are priced to build a sustainable business – not just at a top-line revenue level but at a profit level that enables you to pay yourself what you deserve and cover all necessary business costs. In the next chapter, we will look at how you determine the fee for your services.

CHAPTER 14

PACKAGE AND PRODUCTISE YOUR SERVICES

When it comes to running a successful HR consulting business, one of the most critical decisions you'll make is how to package and price your services. It's tempting to start with an hourly rate, but selling your time isn't necessarily the best approach for long-term success. Instead, think about how to offer value-driven packages and adopt pricing models that reflect the worth of your expertise while also being attractive to clients. A key strategy? Fixed fees and recurring subscription models.

Why? Because clients prefer predictability – they want to know exactly what they're paying for upfront. Fixed fees provide that clarity, while subscription-based services offer a consistent revenue stream for you, which smooths out cash flow and makes your business more resilient.

Let's dive into why this matters and how you can design service packages that are both competitive and profitable.

THE IMPORTANCE OF PACKAGING AND PRICING SERVICES

Packaging and pricing your services aren't just about setting a dollar amount. It's about structuring your offerings in a way that makes sense for both you and your clients. The aim is to create packages that deliver value while simplifying the decision-making process for your clients. People like choices, but they don't want to feel overwhelmed or uncertain about what they're getting.

Many consultants fall into the trap of charging by the hour. While this might seem straightforward, it can lead to challenges for both the consultant and the client. When you charge by the hour, clients don't know exactly how much they'll be billed at the end of the project, which can lead to stress and hesitation. For you, it also sets up a focus on time rather than value.

This is why **fixed-fee pricing** is often a better approach. When you offer a service for a set fee, clients know exactly what they're paying for. It simplifies your sales process and reduces friction in the buying decision. For you, it means you're no longer constrained by the clock, allowing you to focus on delivering exceptional value without worrying about justifying every minute.

Another advantage of fixed fees is that they allow you to **package complementary services together**. This creates a holistic service offering that makes it easier to sell, especially when clients are looking for comprehensive solutions to their HR challenges. This also means that you're able to provide maximum value by strategically addressing all areas of need rather than just one discreet area that does not achieve the desired impact because there are still problems elsewhere.

The **recurring subscription model** takes this one step further. By offering ongoing services for a monthly or yearly fee, you can stabilise your cash flow and provide continuous value to clients. This is a great option for services like HR compliance audits, leadership coaching or ongoing HR support. Clients appreciate the peace of mind that comes with knowing they have access to your services whenever they need them, and you benefit from steady, predictable revenue.

HOW HARRISONS CREATED ITS SERVICE PACKAGES

At Harrisons, we've refined our approach to packaging and pricing over the years, and it's made a huge difference to the business. Early on, like many consultants, I charged clients on an hourly or project-by-project basis. While it worked to an extent, I found it exhausting having to go back to clients every time I needed more hours or a new project agreement. It was inefficient, unpredictable and often led to uncomfortable conversations about money.

That's when I decided to shift to a fixed-fee model for the majority of our services. For example, we offer an HR Compliance Package that includes a range of essential services for a fixed fee. Clients love it because they know exactly what they're paying for each month, and we love it because it simplifies the relationship and also because the client is getting everything they need to be compliant. We don't have to constantly renegotiate or re-estimate. It's a win-win.

We also offer **recurring subscription models** for our more comprehensive services. For instance, clients can subscribe to our HR Team, which includes ongoing HR consulting, quarterly strategy reviews and a set number of hours of support each week. This model provides consistent revenue for the business, and it allows us to hire permanent employees because we have a predictable income stream.

The benefits of these models are enormous:

- **Holistic service offering** – clients appreciate getting everything they need in one package, rather than having to piece together different services from different providers.
- **No need to ask for more money** – once the package is sold, there's no need for constant renegotiation. The client knows exactly what they're paying for and what they'll receive.

- **Smooth revenue stream** – subscription services create consistent cash flow, which is critical for budgeting, growth and hiring.
- **Simplicity** – it's easier to sell a service once and continue delivering value than to keep going back to clients for more projects.

This approach has helped us grow and scale while ensuring we maintain strong, long-lasting relationships with our clients.

HOW TO PACKAGE AND PRICE YOUR SERVICES PROFITABLY

Now, let's look at the five steps necessary to design your own service packages and set pricing strategies that reflect the value you provide while staying competitive.

1. WHAT SERVICES MAKE SENSE TO PACKAGE TOGETHER?

Start by looking at your service offerings. What do your clients need the most, and which services complement each other? Think about creating bundles that solve your clients' problems comprehensively. For example, if you offer HR compliance audits, you might bundle that with contracts, policies and position descriptions. These are services that naturally go hand in hand and deliver greater value together.

The key is to create packages that offer a complete solution. When clients see that you've thought through their needs and packaged services accordingly, it builds trust and makes it easier for them to say yes.

2. CAN YOU ADD EXTRA VALUE?

Another great way to package services is by adding value without adding significant cost to yourself. Think about what else you can offer your clients that enhances the value of the package but doesn't require a lot of extra effort or resources.

For example, you might include access to webinars, download-able templates or exclusive content as part of your service offering.

Clients will perceive this as added value, but for you, it's a way to further differentiate your packages without a significant increase in your time or costs.

3. CAN YOU PUT A FIXED FEE ON THESE SERVICES?

Fixed-fee pricing is all about estimating how long it will take to deliver your services and then setting a price that reflects both your time and the value you provide. While it might feel risky at first, the more you do it, the easier it becomes to estimate.

To get started, look at how many hours similar projects have taken in the past. Factor in your hourly rate, but also consider the market value of the service. What are competitors charging? What is the perceived value to the client? From there, you can set a fixed fee that both covers your costs and offers attractive value to your clients.

Setting your fee at the lower end of your estimate might help you win more work, but it risks undercutting your profit-ability and devaluing your expertise. On the other hand, pricing too high may mean losing potential clients to competitors, but when you do win work, it ensures a healthy profit margin and reinforces the perceived value of your services. The key is finding a balance – pricing confidently to reflect both your worth and what the market can sustain.

4. SETTING YOUR FEES: VALUING YOUR EXPERTISE AND TIME

Pricing your services effectively means striking a balance between reflecting the true value of your expertise and staying competi-tive in the market. This involves more than just calculating your hours – it's about recognising the worth of your knowledge, the years of experience you bring to the table and the results you deliver for your clients. (For a deeper dive into structuring your pricing for profitability, see Chapter 23: Profitable Pricing: Value Your Value.)

To set your fees, start by valuing your expertise. Ask yourself:

- What is the impact of the services you're offering?
- How do your skills and experience translate to value for your clients?
- What would it cost your clients to solve their HR challenges without your help?

It's essential to factor in your business costs and desired profit margin. Don't undersell yourself by only covering costs – your fees should reflect your business expenses (such as software, overheads and team salaries) plus a profit that allows you to grow and reinvest in your business.

Next, research the market rates. This doesn't mean you should undercut the competition, but understanding what others charge helps you position yourself appropriately. If your services are premium, your fees should reflect that. But remember, higher fees need to be backed up by the value you deliver.

Here's a simple formula for setting your fees:

1. Estimate the number of hours it will take to deliver the service.
2. Multiply by your hourly rate (even if you aren't charging hourly, this helps guide your fixed fee).
3. Add a margin for on-costs, profit and unforeseen challenges.
4. Cross-check against market rates to ensure your pricing is competitive.

5. CAN YOU OFFER A RECURRING SUBSCRIPTION MODEL?

One of the best ways to stabilise your income and provide ongoing value to clients is through a subscription model. This is ideal for services that require regular, ongoing support, such as compliance reviews, leadership training or HR strategy development.

Think about how often your clients need your services. Could they benefit from monthly or quarterly check-ins? Are there ongoing tasks you could bundle into a recurring package? For example, ongoing HR advisory services, regular performance reviews or even leadership coaching can all be delivered on a subscription basis. This not only provides value to the client but also guarantees consistent cash flow for your business.

CHECKLIST – PACKAGING SERVICES

As you develop your packages and pricing strategies, use this checklist to ensure you're on the right track.

Identify services that complement each other
Group related services together to create holistic, value-driven packages that solve clients' problems comprehensively.

Ensure your pricing reflects value and market expectations
Set fees based on the impact of your services, your expertise, business costs, and competitive market rates to position yourself effectively.

Incorporate added value without adding significant cost
Enhance your packages by including resources like templates, webinars or exclusive content that provide additional value without requiring extra time investment.

Structure pricing around fixed fees for clarity and consistency
Move away from hourly billing and set clear, fixed fees that provide certainty for both you and your clients while reinforcing the value of your services.

Develop a recurring subscription model
Explore opportunities to create ongoing, subscription-based services that provide long-term value to clients while ensuring a steady revenue stream for your business.

Test and refine your offerings
Pilot your packages with select clients, gather feedback and refine them based on what resonates best with your audience.

Make it easy for clients to choose a package
Ensure your service offerings are simple, clear and tailored to client needs, avoiding overwhelming choices that lead to indecision.

Align pricing with business growth goals
Review and adjust your pricing strategy regularly to reflect your evolving expertise, client demand and financial objectives.

Creating the right service packages and pricing strategies is one of the most important decisions you'll make as a business owner. By focusing on fixed fees and subscription models, you simplify your sales process, provide greater value to your clients and ensure consistent revenue for your business. Take the time to think through your packages and price them based on the value you deliver. This approach will set you up for long-term success and help you build a consulting business that thrives well into the future.

PART 4

IDENTITY

PART 4 - IDENTITY

If you'd told me in the early days of Harrisons that building a brand, marketing and selling would become not only my primary focus but also something I truly enjoy, I wouldn't have believed you. Back then, the thought of "selling" made me cringe. I had the typical "salesman" image in my head of being pushy or convincing people to buy something they may not need - something that felt completely at odds with my skills and values. But over time, I realised that sales isn't about pushing; it's about connecting. Building trust, having honest conversations and exploring where I can add value.

The biggest mindset shift for me came when I embraced the idea that sales is simply about relationships. I love learning about people - their businesses, challenges and journeys. Once I reframed sales as an opportunity to connect, rather than just close deals, it became something I could not only manage but thrive in. And as the business owner, I've learned that no-one can sell Harrisons better than me because I live and breathe our purpose every day. That realisation freed me to focus on what I do best while relying on my incredible team to deliver our services.

This section is all about building an identity that resonates and sells. We'll explore how to create a brand - both personal and business - that aligns with your values and stands out to your ideal clients. We'll look at creating a marketing strategy that works for you and a sales process that's not only structured but also authentic. Whether you're just starting or scaling, these insights will help you create meaningful connections and turn those connections into loyal clients. Because when your identity is clear and your approach is genuine, everything else falls into place.

Many people confuse marketing and sales, but they serve distinct roles in building a successful business. Marketing is about attraction - it's the strategy you use to create awareness, build credibility and engage potential clients before they even consider working with you. It includes branding, content creation, social media, networking and email campaigns - all designed to position you as a trusted expert in your field. Sales, on the other hand, is about conversion - turning those interested prospects into paying clients. Sales involves direct conversations, proposals, negotiations and follow-ups to help potential clients make the decision to buy. Think of marketing as planting seeds and nurturing relationships, while sales is about harvesting the opportunities when the time is right. Both are essential, and when done well, they complement each other seamlessly. In the following chapters, we'll dive into branding, marketing and sales to help you build a business that naturally attracts and wins the right clients.

Identity is about creating and promoting your business and personal brand to attract and retain clients.

CHAPTER 15

CREATE A BRAND THAT RESONATES AND SELLS

Building a successful HR consulting business isn't just about delivering great services – it's also about creating a brand that resonates with your target audience. Whether you realise it or not, your brand is how people perceive your business and you as its leader. It's the promise you make to your clients, and it shapes the way they feel about your services, your values and your company as a whole.

A strong brand identity sets you apart from your competitors and creates an emotional connection with your clients. It encompasses everything from your business name and logo to your tone of voice and the values you communicate. And in today's competitive market, both your business brand and your personal brand are crucial.

So, let's dive into what a brand really is, why it's important, and how you can craft a brand identity that resonates with your audience.

WHAT IS A BRAND AND WHY IS IT IMPORTANT?
Your brand is much more than a logo or tagline. It's the **perception** people have of your business. It's how they feel when they interact with you or your team, the impression your marketing materials leave on them, and the values they associate with your business. It's the story that you tell about who you are and what you stand for.

A brand is particularly important for HR consultants because you're in a people-centric business. Clients are trusting you with their most important resource – their people – and they need to feel a sense of confidence, trust and connection. A strong brand helps build that trust and fosters long-term relationships.

There are two aspects of branding you need to focus on:

- **Personal brand** – as a business owner, your personal brand is just as important as your company's brand. People want to know who they are working with, especially in a consultancy role. Your personal brand is how you present yourself to clients, whether through speaking engagements, networking or social media. It's about being authentic and showing that you are the person behind the company – someone they can trust and relate to.
- **Business brand** – this is how your company is perceived in the market. It includes everything from your business name and logo to your messaging and visual identity, including website, LinkedIn page and social media channels. A strong business brand will communicate professionalism, trustworthiness and the unique value you offer.

PERSONAL BRAND

Your personal brand is about *you* – your values, personality, expertise and the unique traits that make you who you are. It's the perception people have of you as an individual. This includes:

- **Focus** – a personal brand centres on your personal identity and how you present yourself to the world
- **Purpose** – to build trust, credibility and influence as an individual, regardless of the business you own or work for
- **Audience** – it includes colleagues, industry peers, clients and anyone in your professional or personal network.

Consider these elements:
- **Your voice, tone and values** – how you present yourself in person and online
- **Thought leadership and expertise** – the content you develop and share

- **Online presence** – for example, LinkedIn, social media, speaking engagements
- **Your reputation** – how people describe you.

For example, as an HR consultant, your personal brand might focus on being approachable, knowledgeable and committed to fostering workplace wellbeing.

After starting my business, I started writing thought leadership pieces, speaking at events and conferences, and connecting with people on LinkedIn. At first, it felt intimidating, but over time, I began to enjoy it. These activities not only showcased my expertise but also helped me connect with like-minded professionals who shared my passion for HR and business.

Developing my personal brand as a professional and relatable thought leader played a crucial role in Harrisons' growth. As the face of the business, I make a point of being visible at industry events, speaking on panels, presenting webinars and sharing insights through social media. This helps maintain my brand as a thought leader in the HR space and build credibility with clients.

BUSINESS BRAND

A business brand is about *the company* – its identity, mission and what it stands for. It's the image and reputation your company projects to its clients and the market. This includes:

- **Focus** – a business brand focuses on the identity and perception of the business
- **Purpose** – to attract and retain clients, differentiate your services from competitors and establish trust in the market
- **Audience** – primarily clients, potential employees and other stakeholders.

Consider these elements:

- company name, logo, tagline and design elements
- mission, vision and values
- products and services
- client experience and reputation.

HOW HARRISONS BUILT THEIR BRAND

At Harrisons, when I first started I didn't give much thought to branding beyond getting a logo, website and business cards made up. Like many new business owners, I was focused on delivering services and getting clients through the door. But as we grew, I realised that branding was about more than simply having a professional-looking logo – it was about building an identity that resonated with our target audience and reflected who we were as a business.

That's when I decided to get intentional about our brand. I asked myself: What do we want clients to think of when they hear our name? What values are important to us? How can we communicate our unique approach to HR consulting?

I decided that our focus would be working with small to medium-sized businesses that wanted more than just transactional HR support – they wanted a partner in their business growth. So, we positioned ourselves with the vision of *Best Team Best Business* reflecting our commitment to long-term relationships and proactive HR strategy. We also updated our visual identity, making sure our logo, website and marketing materials all conveyed the professionalism and warmth we wanted to be known for.

The result? A more focused, cohesive brand that resonated with our target audience and made it easier to attract and retain clients.

HOW TO CREATE A BUSINESS BRAND THAT RESONATES

Now that we've covered the importance of branding, let's break down the five steps to develop a brand identity that resonates with your audience.

1. DEFINE YOUR BRAND'S PURPOSE AND VALUES

Your brand starts with your purpose – why you exist as a business. This is closely tied to your vision and values, but it also goes deeper into the emotional connection you want to make with clients. What impact do you want to have on their businesses? Why do you do what you do?

Next, define your core values. These are the principles that guide how you run your business. For example, at Harrisons, our values include acting with integrity, delighting the client and backing our team. These values shape every interaction we have with clients and form the foundation of our brand.

2. UNDERSTAND YOUR TARGET AUDIENCE

To create a brand that resonates, you need to know exactly who you're trying to reach. Who are your ideal clients? What challenges do they face? What are their pain points? And how can your services solve their problems?

By understanding your target audience's needs and motivations, you can tailor your brand messaging to speak directly to them. This not only helps attract the right clients but also builds trust and credibility because you're showing that you understand their world.

3. CREATE YOUR VISUAL IDENTITY

Your visual identity includes your logo, colour scheme, fonts and overall design aesthetic. These elements should be consistent across all your marketing materials – from your website and business cards to social media and email newsletters.

When creating your visual identity, think about what message you want to convey. Do you want to come across as modern and innovative or traditional and trustworthy? The colours, fonts and imagery you choose should reflect the tone and values of your business.

At Harrisons, we chose a modern but professional logo and colour palette to communicate both trust and innovation. We have recently updated our logo and website to refresh and modernise our brand. This was important for aligning to our business vision and in positioning ourselves as approachable yet serious about delivering results around people and purpose.

4. CRAFT YOUR BRAND MESSAGING

Your brand messaging is how you communicate your value proposition to clients. This includes your tagline, website copy and the way you talk about your business in client meetings, presentations, on social media and in marketing materials.

When crafting your messaging, focus on the benefits you provide and how you solve your clients' problems. Use clear, concise language that resonates with your target audience. Avoid jargon and industry buzzwords that may confuse or alienate potential clients.

5. BUILD YOUR PERSONAL BRAND

Your business brand messaging should reflect both your business brand and your personal brand. Clients want to feel a connection with you as the business owner, so don't be afraid to let your personality shine through your personal brand.

As the owner of an HR consulting business, your personal brand is just as important as your business brand. Clients want to work with someone they trust, and that trust often comes from knowing the person behind the business.

To build your personal brand, focus on visibility and authenticity. Share your insights and experiences on social media, speak at industry events and network within your community. The more you put yourself out there, the more people will begin to associate you with your expertise and the values you stand for.

Remember, your personal brand should align with your business brand but will also reflect your individual personality. At Harrisons, I made sure that my personal brand as a thought leader complemented the company's identity as a trusted HR partner.

CHECKLIST - BRAND BUILDING

As you develop your brand, use this checklist to ensure you're on the right track.

Define your purpose and values
Clearly articulate why your business exists and the core values that guide your decisions and interactions. ☐

Understand your audience
Identify your ideal clients, their biggest challenges, and how your services solve their problems. ☐

Create a consistent visual identity
Ensure your logo, colour scheme, fonts and design elements are professional, cohesive, and aligned with your brand personality. ☐

Craft compelling brand messaging
Develop a clear, engaging brand message that communicates your value proposition and resonates with your audience. ☐

Build your personal brand
Position yourself as a trusted expert through thought leadership, networking and consistent online and offline visibility. ☐

Align your business and personal brand
Ensure your personal brand complements your business brand while showcasing your expertise, personality and leadership. ☐

Establish a strong online presence
Optimise your website, LinkedIn profile, and social media channels to reflect your brand identity and attract ideal clients. ☐

Be visible and engaged in your industry
Attend events, speak on panels, publish content and actively engage in discussions to build credibility and expand your reach. ☐

Ensure brand consistency across all touchpoints
Maintain a unified look, tone and message across your website, social media, emails, proposals and client communications. ☐

Review and refine your brand regularly
Periodically assess your branding to ensure it stays relevant, professional and aligned with your business growth and goals. ☐

Creating a brand that resonates with your audience is one of the most powerful ways to differentiate yourself in the HR consulting space. By defining your purpose, understanding your audience and crafting a strong, cohesive identity, you'll attract the right clients and build long-lasting relationships.

Your brand is more than just a logo or a name – it's the experience, trust and emotional connection you create with your clients. By being intentional about both your business and personal brand, you'll position yourself for success and establish a lasting impact in the market.

Your brand is just one essential component of your overall marketing strategy, which we will explore in the next chapter.

CHAPTER 16

YOUR ESSENTIAL MARKETING GAME PLAN

Building a successful HR consulting business isn't just about offering great services – it's about making sure potential clients know who you are and what you can do for them. This is where your marketing strategy comes into play. Without a solid plan to get the word out, even the best HR consultants can struggle to attract the clients they need to grow. Marketing, especially for a start-up, is how you connect with your audience, communicate your value and ultimately attract prospects who are converted into paying clients.

One key principle to remember when marketing your HR consulting services is the "rule of 7", which is that a potential client typically needs to encounter a brand's message at least seven times before making a purchase decision, meaning it takes around seven "touches" to convert them into a buyer. This rule underscores the importance of consistent, multi-channel marketing. Clients need to hear from you, see your content and feel engaged with your brand multiple times before they are ready to trust you with their HR needs.

So, a one-off ad or post won't cut it. You need a well-thought-out, continuous strategy that engages clients at various touch-points.

THE IMPORTANCE OF A MARKETING STRATEGY FOR HR CONSULTING START-UPS

For an HR consulting start-up, getting your name out there is one of the most critical steps to success. In a crowded market, it's not enough to rely on word-of-mouth or occasional social media posts. You need a strategy that builds your brand, generates qualified leads and keeps your business top of mind for potential clients.

A marketing strategy helps you:

- **Increase visibility** – it ensures that your target audience knows who you are and what you do. Without visibility, you can't build trust or relationships with potential clients.
- **Build credibility** – by consistently sharing valuable insights and demonstrating your expertise, you establish yourself as a trusted expert in the HR space.
- **Generate leads** – a strong marketing plan will bring in a steady stream of qualified leads, so you aren't constantly scrambling for new business.
- **Drive engagement** – engaging your audience through multiple channels creates familiarity, and as the "rule of 7" shows, familiarity breeds trust – and eventually, conversions.

Your marketing plan should align with your overall business goals, ensuring that every effort you put into marketing is driving growth. Let's explore how you can create a marketing game plan that attracts and retains clients.

HOW HARRISONS APPROACHES MARKETING

At Harrisons, our marketing strategy has been a cornerstone of our growth. I've learned that a well-planned, consistent marketing effort helps to create a pipeline of qualified leads and makes it easier to convert prospects into long-term clients.

Our marketing approach is built around two key elements:

- **An annual high-level marketing plan** – this plan is aligned with our overall business plan and helps ensure that our marketing efforts support our long-term business goals. It includes high-level objectives, such as increasing brand awareness, generating leads and nurturing existing clients.
- **A detailed marketing calendar** – to support our annual plan, we use a marketing calendar with monthly themes and content. Each month has a specific content focus and a call to action (CTA), allowing us to maintain consistency and ensure that we're always delivering valuable, relevant content to our audience. This calendar keeps us organised and focused, ensuring that our marketing efforts are not only frequent but also aligned with our business objectives.

We've found that **multi-modal marketing** – using a variety of channels to reach our audience – has been critical to our success. For us, the focus is on:

- **LinkedIn** – since we are a B2B (business-to-business) HR consultancy, LinkedIn is a key platform for us. It's where our target audience spends time, making it the ideal place to share industry insights, thought leadership articles and updates on our services.
- **EDMs (Electronic Direct Mail)** – we send regular email newsletters to our database of contacts, sharing valuable content like HR tips, updates on employment law and links to upcoming webinars. This helps us stay top of mind with our clients and prospects.
- **Online events** – webinars and virtual workshops have been a great way for us to engage with our audience, showcase our expertise and build trust with potential clients.
- **In-person events** – we attend and present at a range of events, including partner breakfasts, industry events and business networking.

A critical component of our marketing strategy has been investing in a CRM (Customer Relationship Management) system. Our CRM helps us manage our contact database, track leads and automate nurturing sequences. These nurturing sequences – emails that are automatically sent to prospects over time – keep our leads warm and engaged, even if they aren't ready to buy right away.

By building premium content like guides, eBooks and white papers, we offer value upfront, positioning ourselves as trusted experts. This helps build relationships and keeps our audience coming back for more. Our CRM also allows us to segment our audience, ensuring that the right people get the right content at the right time. This creates a steady stream of qualified leads that are easier to convert into clients when the time is right.

HOW TO CREATE YOUR MARKETING GAME PLAN

Now that you've seen how a structured marketing plan can support business growth, let's break down the seven steps to creating your own comprehensive marketing strategy.

1. DEFINE YOUR MARKETING OBJECTIVES

Start by setting clear objectives for your marketing efforts. What do you want to achieve? Your marketing goals should align with your business goals. Common marketing objectives for an HR consulting start-up might include:

- increasing brand awareness within your target market
- generating a consistent flow of qualified leads
- nurturing existing leads to move them through your sales funnel
- establishing yourself as a thought leader in the HR industry.

By having a clear understanding of your goals, you can tailor your marketing efforts to achieve these specific outcomes.

2. UNDERSTAND YOUR CLIENT AVATAR

Refer back to the Niche section on the importance of defining and understanding your client avatar. When developing marketing content, always imagine that you're talking with that client avatar.

Give your avatar a name and photo, like *Sarah the Law Firm Owner* or *Mark the HR Manager* and use it whenever you're creating marketing materials to stay focused on their needs. The clearer you are about who you serve, the easier it will be to attract the right clients and grow your HR consulting business with confidence.

3. DEVELOP A MULTI-CHANNEL APPROACH

To reach potential clients across multiple touch-points, it's important to leverage a variety of channels in your marketing plan. Here are some key channels to consider:

- **Social media** – platforms like LinkedIn are powerful tools for B2B businesses. There are other platforms that may be better suited to your client avatar. Use social media to share valuable insights, post regular updates and engage with your audience. Make sure your posts align with your monthly content themes and offer actionable advice or thought leadership in HR consulting.

- **Email marketing** – build and maintain a database of contacts by sending regular email newsletters or EDMs. Focus on providing value – whether it's helpful HR tips, updates on industry trends or promoting your services. Emails help nurture relationships over time, especially for clients who aren't ready to make a decision right away.

- **Content marketing** – create and share premium content that demonstrates your expertise. This could include blog posts, white papers, case studies or webinars. The goal is to provide your audience with valuable insights that position you as a trusted expert in HR consulting.

- **Events and webinars** – host online events, such as webinars or virtual workshops, to showcase your expertise and engage directly with potential clients. These events allow you to provide in-depth information and build relationships in a more interactive setting.

- **Online advertising** – advertising online can be a powerful tool for HR consultants, but it needs to be carefully managed to avoid wasted spend. Treat online ads as part of your overall marketing strategy – not the only strategy.

A balanced approach with ads, organic marketing and relationship-building will deliver the best long-term results.

4. EXPAND YOUR MARKETING STRATEGY WITH RELATIONSHIP BUILDING

A comprehensive marketing plan goes beyond digital and networking event strategies and should include proactive relationship-building approaches. Here's how you can enhance your marketing game plan:

- **Start with Who you Know** – as a start-up consulting business, the easiest way to win business is by utilising your existing network. Make a list of everyone you know professionally and personally. Let them know you've started your business and are looking for clients. Follow up key opportunities with calls and catch-ups.

- **Get out to Market Personally** – actively market both your business and yourself. Personal networking and one-on-one meetings are essential for building genuine relationships and trust. Attend networking events, conferences and industry meet-ups to create face-to-face connections with potential clients and referrers.

- **Partnerships and Referrer Arrangements** – establishing partnerships and referral networks can significantly extend your reach. Partner with complementary businesses such as accounting firms or business coaches who serve similar audiences. Consider setting up formal referral agreements where both parties benefit from recommending each other's services.

- **Public Relations (PR)** – leverage PR strategies to build brand authority. Write thought leadership articles, participate in industry panels and engage with media opportunities.

PR helps position you as a credible expert while expanding your visibility to new audiences.

5. CREATE A DETAILED MARKETING CALENDAR

To ensure consistency and keep your marketing efforts organised, develop a marketing calendar. This should outline your monthly content themes, key messages and the specific channels you'll use to distribute that content. A well-structured calendar helps you stay on track and ensures that you're always engaging with your audience in a meaningful way.

At Harrisons, we use a high-level annual plan to set broad goals and then drill down into a more detailed calendar that outlines our content and calls to action (CTAs) for each month. This approach allows us to maintain focus while being flexible enough to adjust to changes in the market or client needs.

6. BUILD A CRM-DRIVEN NURTURING SEQUENCE

A CRM system is an invaluable tool for managing your marketing efforts, especially when it comes to nurturing leads. Once you've attracted potential clients through your marketing efforts, it's important to keep them engaged even if they aren't ready to buy immediately.

By setting up automated nurturing sequences, you can stay in touch with leads over time, offering them valuable content and keeping your business top of mind. These sequences are often triggered by specific actions, like downloading a white paper or attending a webinar, and can help guide leads through the decision-making process.

Your CRM can also help you track engagement, so you know when a lead is ready to move to the next stage of the sales funnel. This makes it easier to convert leads into paying clients when the time is right.

7. MONITOR AND MEASURE YOUR MARKETING SUCCESS

Great marketing isn't just about launching campaigns – it's about understanding whether those efforts are generating the right results. Without tracking performance, you won't know what's working, what's not, or where to focus your time and resources.

To effectively measure your marketing, you need to track both lead indicators and lag indicators:

- Marketing lead indicators measure the activities and efforts that build brand awareness and attract potential clients. These metrics help you assess whether you're on the right track before results start to show.
- Marketing lag indicators measure the actual outcomes of your marketing efforts, such as new clients signed or revenue generated. These numbers tell you whether your marketing strategy is ultimately working.

This chapter focuses on marketing indicators, which track how well you're attracting interest in your services. In the next chapter, we'll explore sales indicators, which measure how effectively you're converting that interest into paying clients.

MARKETING LEAD INDICATORS: PREDICTIVE METRICS

Lead indicators help you assess whether your marketing activities are building momentum and likely to generate future clients. These are early signals that indicate progress, even before they turn into revenue.

Examples of marketing lead indicators:

- number of LinkedIn posts published this month
- networking events attended
- new email subscribers added
- click-through rates (CTR) on online ads
- engagement levels on social media posts (likes, shares, comments).

If you're consistently creating content, engaging with potential clients and expanding your network, you're laying the foundation for future inquiries and business growth.

MARKETING LAG INDICATORS: OUTCOME METRICS

Lag indicators measure the end results of your marketing efforts. These are performance-based metrics that reflect whether your strategy is delivering tangible business outcomes.

Examples of marketing lag indicators:

- number of new client inquiries from marketing efforts
- revenue generated from marketing campaigns
- conversion rate of website visitors to inquiries
- percentage of leads converted into paying clients
- return on ad spend (ROAS) from paid advertising.

Since lag indicators only show results after the fact, they are useful for evaluating your overall marketing success and adjusting your strategy accordingly.

HOW TO MEASURE YOUR MARKETING PERFORMANCE

A structured approach to tracking and measuring marketing success helps ensure your efforts are effective. Here's a simple five-step process:

1. **Set clear marketing goals** – What does success look like? (e.g., Increase LinkedIn engagement by 30% or generate 10 new client inquiries per month.)
2. **Choose key lead and lag indicators** – Identify specific metrics that align with your goals.
3. **Track performance consistently** – Use a CRM, Google Analytics, LinkedIn Insights or a spreadsheet to monitor progress.
4. **Review and analyse monthly** – Identify trends and patterns. What's working? What's underperforming?
5. **Refine your strategy** – Adjust your focus based on data. If webinars are driving more inquiries than networking events, shift your efforts accordingly.

By tracking and analysing marketing performance regularly, you'll be able to refine your strategy, invest in the right activities, and confidently grow your HR consulting business.

MARKETING FOR START-UPS AND SOLO CONSULTANTS

When you're running a solo consulting business, marketing often feels like an overwhelming extra task – especially when you're already busy delivering services. The challenge is real: how do you consistently bring in new clients while managing the work you already have? The key is focusing on high-impact activities that provide the best return on your time and money.

When I started my business, I didn't have a big marketing budget or a dedicated team – I was the business. So, I had to be strategic about where I put my energy. I focused on building relationships and getting visible with my prospective clients, because in consulting, trust and credibility are everything. Here's what worked for me:

- **Networking and relationship management** – I made it a priority to nurture my existing connections and build new ones. Whether it was former colleagues, industry peers or local business groups, I made sure people knew what I did and how I could help.
- **LinkedIn outreach** – I used LinkedIn to stay top of mind, sharing insights, engaging with potential clients and sending personalised messages to those in my network to organise coffee catch-ups.
- **Partner referrals** – I built relationships with accountants, lawyers, business coaches and other professionals who worked with my ideal clients, offering value to them in return.
- **Speaking and presenting** – I presented at industry events and ran seminars in partnership with others. This positioned me as an expert and gave me direct access to potential clients.
- **Keeping in touch** – I stayed in regular contact with people I had met, checking in, sharing useful information and keeping conversations going – not just when I needed work.
- **Lots of coffees!** – I had countless one-on-one meetings with potential clients, referrers and collaborators. Sometimes, I even had a baby in tow!

If you're a solo consultant or just starting out, the key is prioritising relationship-building activities. You don't need a complex digital marketing strategy in the beginning – focus on human connections, credibility and getting in front of the right people. Over time, as your business grows, you can introduce more structured marketing efforts. But in the early days, showing up, adding value and staying visible is what will get you your first (and next) clients.

CHECKLIST – MARKETING GAME PLAN

Use this checklist to guide the development of your marketing strategy.

Define marketing objectives
Set specific, measurable goals that align with your business growth plans, such as increasing brand awareness, generating qualified leads and nurturing client relationships.

Identify your ideal client
Develop a detailed client avatar outlining your ideal client's challenges, goals and needs to tailor your messaging effectively.

Leverage a multi-channel approach
Use diverse channels like LinkedIn, email marketing, content creation, webinars, in-person events and partnerships to engage with your audience multiple times across different platforms.

Develop a content calendar
Plan your content strategy with monthly themes, key messages and calls to action, ensuring consistent messaging and high-quality marketing output.

Invest in a CRM
Use a Customer Relationship Management (CRM) tool to manage contacts, track leads and automate nurturing sequences to keep your prospects engaged.

Engage in personal marketing efforts
Dedicate time for personal marketing activities like networking, speaking engagements and direct outreach to build trust and credibility with potential clients and referrers.

Establish partnerships and referral networks
Form strategic alliances with complementary service providers, such as accountants, business coaches and industry bodies, to expand your reach and create mutually beneficial referral opportunities.

Utilise PR for authority building
Incorporate public relations strategies such as writing industry articles, speaking at events and engaging media to position yourself as a thought leader in HR consulting.

Monitor and measure performance
Regularly track both lead (such as LinkedIn engagement, email open rates and discovery calls booked) and lag indicators (such as client conversions and revenue growth) to assess the effectiveness of your marketing strategy.

Refine and adapt regularly
Continuously review the success of your marketing efforts, identify areas for improvement and adjust your strategy to align with evolving market trends and client needs.

A well-rounded marketing strategy ensures visibility, builds trust and creates opportunities for sustainable business growth. By consistently applying these principles, you'll establish your HR consulting business as a leader in the market.

The more touch-points you create with your audience, the more familiar they become with your brand, and the more likely they are to trust you when they're ready to make a decision. With a solid marketing strategy in place, you'll not only increase your visibility but also create lasting relationships that drive long-term success for your business.

Now that you have leads rolling in with your awesome marketing strategy, let's consider how you convert those leads into new clients.

CHAPTER 17

CLOSING THE DEAL: TURNING LEADS INTO PAYING CLIENTS

At Harrisons, we've learned that while we may not always love the idea of "sales", it's an essential part of running a successful consulting business. Just as we invest heavily in marketing and brand building, we also dedicate significant effort to actioning our leads and making sure they're nurtured all the way to conversion.

DON'T LEAVE SALES TO CHANCE

To ensure we don't leave sales to chance, we've developed a structured sales system that helps us stay organised and focused. Here's what our seven-step system looks like:

1. **The sales process is mapped** – we've mapped out each step of the sales process, from the moment a lead comes in through marketing activity, all the way to closing the deal. This includes specific actions we take at each stage, like sending an introductory email, scheduling a discovery call or following up after a proposal has been sent.

2. **Template scripts** – to make sure we're consistent in our communications, we use template scripts for key touch-points, such as initial outreach, discovery calls and follow-ups. This helps us maintain a professional and cohesive message across all interactions with potential clients.

3. **CRM database** – all of our contacts and leads are tracked in our CRM (Customer Relationship Management) system. This allows us to manage our pipeline, track conversations, schedule follow-ups and store important information about each lead.
4. **Follow-up monitoring** – follow-up is crucial in the sales process. We track and monitor every follow-up to ensure that no lead is left hanging. Our CRM system sends reminders when it's time to follow up, and we have clear guidelines on how and when to reach out.
5. **Lead nurture sequences** – for leads that aren't ready to buy right away, we have automated nurture sequences in place. These sequences send helpful and relevant content over time, keeping us top of mind and building trust until the lead is ready to move forward.
6. **Proposal templates** – we have standard proposal templates that we can easily customise for each client. This stream-lines the proposal process and ensures that we can respond quickly to opportunities.
7. **Allocated time and responsibilities** – we allocate specific time and resources to sales activities. Everyone on the team knows their role in the process, whether it's managing leads, sending follow-up emails or closing the deal.

Having this system in place has not only made our sales process more efficient, but it's also helped us feel more confident in our ability to close deals without feeling "salesy".

DEVELOPING YOUR STRUCTURED SALES PROCESS

Now, let's dive into how you can develop a structured sales process for your HR consulting business. The key is to break down your sales funnel into manageable steps and ensure you have clear strategies for each of the three stages: lead generation, nurturing and closing.

1. LEAD GENERATION

The first step in any sales process is generating leads, which was mostly covered in the previous chapter on marketing strategy. Generating leads involves attracting potential clients who are interested in your services and getting them into your sales funnel. Following are the various methods of lead generation we've used at Harrisons:

- **Networking** – whether it's in-person at industry events or online through platforms like LinkedIn, networking is a great way to generate leads. Build relationships with potential clients and industry influencers to create opportunities for new business.
- **Content marketing** – sharing valuable content, such as blog posts, webinars, client testimonials or case studies, can attract potential clients to your website and encourage them to reach out for more information.
- **Referral programs** – encourage your current employees and clients to refer you to potential clients (and employees). Often, the best leads come from word-of-mouth recommendations from satisfied clients and engaged employees.
- **Lead magnets** – offer something of value in exchange for contact information. This could be a free eBook, a guide or access to a webinar, all of which can help you capture leads and start the nurturing process. At Harrisons, we send a copy of my first book, *The CEO Secret Guide to Managing and Motivating Employees* to strong leads.

2. LEAD NURTURING

Once you have a lead in your system, the next step is nurturing that lead until they're ready to become a client. This is where you build trust and demonstrate your value with:

- **Follow-up emails** – after an initial conversation, send a follow-up email to thank the lead for their time and provide any additional information or resources they may need.
- **Educational content** – send helpful content that addresses their specific challenges or questions. This could be articles, case studies or testimonials from other clients.
- **Discovery calls** – schedule a discovery call to better understand their needs and see how your services can help them. This is a crucial step in building a relationship and moving the lead closer to making a decision.

- **Stay top of mind** – use your CRM system to keep track of leads and schedule periodic check-ins. Even if they're not ready to buy immediately, staying in touch keeps you top of mind for when they are.

3. CLOSING STRATEGIES

The final step in the sales process is **closing the deal**. This is where you convert the lead into a paying client with:

- **Proposal presentations** – when presenting your proposal, focus on the value you'll deliver. Highlight how your services will solve their problems and help them achieve their goals.
- **Handling objections** – be prepared to handle objections. Whether it's about price, timing or other concerns, address objections calmly and confidently, and reinforce the value you provide.
- **Create urgency** – encourage prospects to take action by creating a sense of urgency. This could be offering a limited-time discount or emphasising the benefits of getting started sooner rather than later.
- **Close with confidence** – when the time comes, ask for the business directly. Be confident in your value and don't hesitate to ask for the sale. This includes follow-up calls.

4. SETTING AND MONITORING SALES TARGETS

Tracking and measuring your sales performance is essential to maintaining steady business growth. By setting Sales Key Performance Indicators (KPIs), you can stay focused, measure progress and make data-driven adjustments to improve your results.

The most effective way to monitor sales performance is by balancing lead indicators (sales activities within your control) with lag indicators (the outcomes of those activities).

SALES LEAD INDICATORS: ACTIVITIES YOU CONTROL

Lead indicators track the sales actions you take that influence future results. These metrics provide early insights into whether you're taking enough action to generate sales before results materialise.

Examples of sales lead indicators:
- number of sales calls made
- networking events attended
- discovery meetings booked
- proposals sent
- follow-up emails or calls completed.

Consistent lead activities drive future revenue. If your sales activity slows down, so will your results.

SALES LAG INDICATORS: MEASURING SALES OUTCOMES

Lag indicators measure the results of your sales efforts. They help assess whether your strategy is effective, but since they reflect past performance, they don't allow for immediate course correction.

Examples of sales lag indicators:
- number of new clients signed
- total revenue generated
- proposal-to-client conversion rate
- average deal size
- client retention rate.

Lag indicators help determine whether you're meeting your sales goals, but to improve outcomes, you need to adjust your lead activities.

SETTING AND TRACKING YOUR SALES KPIs

To effectively track sales performance, follow these five steps:

1. **Define clear revenue targets** – Start with a realistic revenue goal, then break it down into monthly and weekly sales targets. Example: If your goal is $240K per year, that may mean two new clients per month based on your average service fee.

2. **Select key lead and lag indicators** – Choose three to five lead indicators (such as calls made and meetings booked) and three to five lag indicators (such as new clients signed).

3. **Track consistently** – Use a CRM system, sales tracker or spreadsheet to log activity and monitor results over time.

4. **Review and adjust regularly** – Set aside time each month to review your sales KPIs. If you're not hitting revenue targets, increase lead activities or refine your approach.
5. **Stay accountable** – Whether you track solo or with a mentor, keeping your sales performance visible and measurable helps maintain focus and consistency.

Sales is a numbers game. The more calls, meetings and follow-ups you complete, the better your results will be. Track progress weekly so you can adjust early rather than react to a slow quarter.

By consistently monitoring your sales KPIs, you'll develop a structured, repeatable approach to winning new clients and growing your HR consulting business with confidence.

SALES IN A SOLO BUSINESS

When you're running a solo business, sales can feel overwhelming, but it's just as important – if not more so – when you're the only one responsible for driving revenue. The key is to keep things simple and manageable. Start by dedicating specific time each week to sales activities, whether that's following up with leads, sending out proposals or scheduling discovery calls. Consistency is critical, even when you're juggling client work.

Use your CRM (or spreadsheet) to keep track of prospects and ensure you don't let any opportunities slip through the cracks. Automate what you can, like follow-up emails or nurturing sequences, to keep leads warm without spending too much time on manual tasks. Remember, sales doesn't have to be aggressive; it's about building relationships and showing potential clients the value you bring. Even as a solo consultant, having a structured sales process will help you stay on top of opportunities and close deals without feeling overwhelmed.

CHECKLIST - SALES SUCCESS

Once you have a solid marketing strategy in place and leads are coming in, the next critical step is converting those leads into paying clients. A well-defined sales process ensures that your efforts in marketing translate into actual business growth. Below is an action-oriented checklist to help you build and refine your sales process effectively.

Develop your sales plan and set clear targets
Create a structured sales plan, including defined targets and KPIs. Monitor both lead and lag indicators on a weekly basis.

Implement a lead generation strategy
Establish a clear approach for generating consistent leads, such as networking, content marketing, referrals and lead magnets.

Set up and use a CRM system effectively
Implement a CRM to track leads, follow-ups and client information. Use it to manage your sales pipeline and keep data organised.

Create automated lead nurture sequences
Develop automated email sequences that provide value and keep leads engaged over time, ensuring they stay connected until ready to buy.

Monitor and maintain follow-ups consistently
Schedule regular follow-ups with all leads to keep conversations progressing. Ensure follow-ups are timely and relevant to prospect's needs.

Prepare professional proposal templates
Design ready-to-use proposal templates that are easily customised for each lead. Ensure they are clear, visually appealing, and aligned with your brand.

Refine your objection handling techniques
Prepare strategies to address common objections and rehearse responses to build confidence when closing deals.

Master closing techniques
Develop and practise multiple closing strategies to help you confidently ask for the business and secure new clients.

Track sales performance metrics
Regularly review sales performance metrics such as conversion rates, deal size and sales cycle length. Use insights to identify areas for improvement.

Continuously improve and optimise your sales process
Regularly review and refine your sales approach based on performance data and client feedback. Stay updated on best practices and adjust accordingly.

By following this checklist, you will create a streamlined and effective sales process that turns potential leads into loyal clients. Consistent execution and ongoing refinement are key to sustained business growth.

I cannot reiterate enough the importance of developing a structured sales process to convert leads into clients, including lead generation, nurturing and closing strategies. It's very easy to shy away from sales but ignoring it will be detrimental to your business. Without a structured sales process, you risk losing out on potential clients and leaving money on the table. By developing a clear, step-by-step system for lead generation, nurturing and closing, you'll not only increase your conversion rates but also build stronger relationships with your clients. Sales may not be your favourite part of the business, but it's absolutely essential for long-term success.

PART 5

TEAM

PART 5 – TEAM

When I started Harrisons, I wore every hat in the business – HR consultant, marketer, bookkeeper, admin assistant and even IT troubleshooter. It didn't take long to realise that trying to do it all wasn't just exhausting – it was unsustainable. If I wanted to grow, I needed help. Over time, I discovered that building a dream team isn't just about hiring employees; it's about leveraging the right mix of people, tools and systems to support your business. That meant embracing technology and flexible work arrangements, and it's made all the difference.

One of the biggest game-changers has been technology, especially AI. Tools that automate tasks, streamline processes and reduce admin time are a gift to small business owners like us. At Harrisons, we've invested heavily in building our intellectual property – tools, templates, webinars and resources – to make service delivery smoother and more profitable.

By systemising and productising our services, we've not only reduced training time but also improved the consistency and quality of what we deliver. It's amazing what you can achieve when your team is supported by the right tech and a library of well-designed resources.

This section is all about scaling smart. From identifying the right mix of resources – employees, contractors, gig workers or consultants – to embracing tech and AI, we'll explore how to build a team that supports your vision without breaking your budget. Whether you're just starting to grow or looking to fine-tune your operations, these chapters will show you how to scale in a way that's productive, profitable and sustainable. After all, success isn't about doing it all yourself; it's about building the right support network to help you thrive – and achieve that much desired work-life balance.

Team is the basis of your ability to scale your business because you cannot do it alone.

CHAPTER 18

ENGAGE THE RIGHT RESOURCES FOR YOUR BUSINESS

As your HR consulting business grows, it's impossible to do everything on your own forever. Whether you're working solo or planning to build a full team, resourcing is crucial to scaling your business. It's about more than just hiring employees – it involves making strategic decisions about when and how to bring in the right talent to support your business, whether that's full-time employees, contractors, freelancers or outsourced services. The goal is to ensure you have the right resources in place to deliver on your business goals and continue growing sustainably.

This chapter will explore the different ways to resource your business and the steps you need to take to build your dream team. Whether you're a solo consultant looking to offload some tasks or you're planning to build a full team, knowing when and how to add resources is essential for success.

THE IMPORTANCE OF RESOURCING RIGHT
Running a consulting business requires a wide range of skills, from delivering services to managing operations, marketing, finances and client relationships. In the early stages, it's common to wear many hats, but as you start to grow, trying to handle everything yourself becomes unsustainable. This is where **resourcing** comes in.

Adequate resourcing allows you to focus on what you do best – delivering value to your clients – while ensuring that other critical aspects of your business are being managed effectively. Resourcing isn't just about hiring employees. There are many options available, including:

- contractors
- freelancers
- outsourcing
- offshoring.

The right combination of these resources can provide flexibility, cost-efficiency and access to specific expertise that can help you scale your business faster.

HOW HARRISONS BUILT ITS TEAM

At Harrisons, I started as a solo consultant, and like many new business owners, I initially tried to do everything myself. From consulting to admin, marketing and even bookkeeping, it was all on my plate. However, I quickly realised that if I wanted to grow the business, I needed to free up my time to focus on the bigger picture.

At one point, I was working late into the evenings and on weekends, just to keep everything running. My work-life balance was virtually non-existent, and I felt like I was constantly juggling too many things at once. The turning point came when I realised I was spending too much time on tasks that weren't generating revenue – admin, invoicing, not-the-right networking events and managing social media – while the real value I brought to the business was in consulting, strategy and building client relationships. That's when I knew I had to start letting go and delegating, focusing my time on high-impact work that would drive the business forward.

My first hire was another consultant – another revenue generator. This was a crucial step because it allowed me to bring someone on board to deliver client work, which in turn freed me up to focus on growing the business. It wasn't an easy decision at first – paying someone else, letting go of control and trusting someone else to deliver the work was a challenge – but it was absolutely necessary for scaling.

The second role I added was business and client services administrative support. As the business grew, the administrative tasks, from scheduling to client communication, became too much for me to handle on my own. Having someone dedicated to managing these tasks made a huge difference in my day-to-day productivity and allowed me to focus more on strategy and client relationships.

From there, as revenue allowed, I continued to bring on more consultants. These hires are now permanent because I want a committed team that grows with the business and understands the culture of Harrisons. When hiring, I look for more than just technical expertise – I seek people who align with our core values: Delight the Client, Act with Integrity and Back the Team. I want consultants who take ownership of their work, go the extra mile for clients and genuinely care about delivering quality outcomes. Equally important is their commitment to Harrisons and each other – collaborating, supporting one another and contributing to a strong team culture. Hiring the right people isn't just about skills; it's about finding those who share our mindset and approach to doing business.

I've also used offshoring for various tasks that didn't require an in-house team member, such as website development and eLearning course creation. Offshoring gave us access to talented professionals at a lower cost, allowing us to scale certain areas of the business without the expense of hiring employees.

In addition, I've outsourced non-core functions like bookkeeping, accounting and marketing support. For me, it made sense to outsource these areas to experts who could handle them more efficiently, allowing the internal team to focus on our core services.

Finally, I've used contractors for flexibility on set projects. This approach gives us the ability to scale up quickly when needed, without the long-term commitment of a permanent or full-time hire. However, I do prefer hiring permanent employees when possible, as it fosters more commitment to Harrisons and strengthens the team culture.

KEY STEPS FOR IDENTIFYING THE RIGHT RESOURCES

Now that you understand the importance of resourcing and how I've built my team at Harrisons, let's look at the three key steps you should take when planning for your own business.

1. WHAT CAPABILITIES AND RESOURCES DO YOU NEED?

The first step in building your team is identifying the capabilities and resources you need to deliver on your business plan. Start by reviewing your business goals and considering what it will take to achieve them. Ask yourself:

- What services are you offering, and what skills are needed to deliver those services?
- What are your current pain points – areas where you're spending too much time or don't have the expertise?
- What roles could free up your time to focus on strategic growth or client relationships?

For example, if you're spending too much time on administrative tasks, hiring a part-time admin assistant or virtual assistant might be the solution. If your business plan includes expanding into new service areas, you may need to hire consultants with specific expertise in those areas.

2. EXPLORE RESOURCING OPTIONS

Once you know what capabilities you need, it's time to explore the different resourcing options available. Each option has its pros and cons, so it's important to choose the one that best fits your business's needs and budget.

Here are the main options to consider:

- **Employees** – hiring employees gives you the benefit of having dedicated team members who are committed to your business. They are invested in your company's success and can help build a strong team culture. However, employees come with higher costs (salaries, training, benefits, etc.) and are a long-term commitment.

- **Contractors** – contractors are ideal for projects with a defined start and end. They provide flexibility because you can bring them in when needed without committing to long-term employment. The downside is that contractors may not have the same level of investment in your business as employees.

- **Freelancers** – freelancers are similar to contractors but tend to work on shorter, more specific tasks. They are great for areas like content creation, graphic design or social media management. Freelancers offer flexibility and cost savings but may not always be available when you need them.

- **Outsourcing** – outsourcing involves hiring an external company or individual to handle non-core functions like bookkeeping, payroll or marketing. This option can save you time and money while allowing you to focus on your core services. The downside is that you have less control over the quality and timeliness of the work.

- **Offshoring** – offshoring involves hiring talent from overseas, often at a lower cost than hiring locally. This is a great option for tasks like IT development, design or content creation. However, managing an offshore team can come with communication challenges and time zone differences.

- **Virtual Assistant (VA)** – hiring a VA can be a game-changer for keeping your sales and marketing activities consistent while you focus on client work and strategy. This includes:
  - researching potential clients, compiling prospect lists and qualifying leads
  - scheduling social media posts, email campaigns and content distribution

-   following up on enquiries, scheduling meetings and managing your CRM system
-   creating proposals and preparing client documents for you to review and send.

3. HIRE, RETAIN AND FLEX FOR YOUR BUSINESS

Once you've identified the resources you need and chosen the best resourcing options, the next step is to build your team. But it's not just about hiring the right people – it's about retaining them and ensuring your team can flex as your business grows and changes. Consider:

-   **Hiring** – when hiring employees, contractors or freelancers, make sure you have a clear understanding of the skills and attributes you're looking for. Develop job descriptions that outline not only the technical requirements but also the values and behaviours that align with your company culture.
-   **Retention** – to retain your team, invest in creating a positive work environment where team members feel valued and engaged. Offer opportunities for professional development, provide regular feedback and foster a sense of belonging. This is especially important in a consulting business, where your team's expertise and commitment are crucial to client success.
-   **Flexibility** – as your business grows, the needs of your team may change. Be prepared to adjust your resourcing strategy based on evolving business demands. This might mean bringing on more contractors during busy periods or hiring additional employees as revenue allows. Flexibility is key to ensuring that your business can scale without being constrained by your team's capacity.

CHECKLIST – BUILDING YOUR DREAM TEAM

Here's a checklist to help guide you through the process of building your team.

Identify key capabilities
Determine the skills and expertise required to deliver your services effectively and support your business growth.

Explore resourcing options
Assess the benefits and drawbacks of employees, contractors, freelancers, outsourcing, offshoring and virtual assistants to find the right fit for your business.

Plan for flexibility
Ensure your resourcing strategy allows you to scale up or down as needed to adapt to business growth and changing client demands.

Develop clear job descriptions
Define the skills, experience and attributes needed for each role, ensuring alignment with your company culture and business goals.

Use a strategic hiring approach
Prioritise hiring for critical roles first, starting with those that free up your time to focus on revenue-generating activities.

Leverage outsourcing and automation
Identify non-core tasks that can be outsourced or automated to improve efficiency and reduce workload.

Create a strong retention strategy
Invest in professional development, foster a positive work environment and provide regular feedback to retain top talent.

Establish a contractor and freelancer network
Build a reliable pool of external specialists to support your business during peak and holiday periods or for project-based work.

Implement team engagement and support structures
Develop processes for communication, collaboration and performance management to ensure team members stay engaged and productive.

Regularly review and adjust your resourcing plan
Reassess your team structure and needs as your business
evolves to ensure you have the right people and systems in
place.

Resourcing is one of the most critical aspects of growing your
HR consulting business. Whether you're a solo consultant looking
to offload tasks or planning to build a full team, having the right
resources in place is essential for delivering value to your clients
and scaling your business for financial freedom and flexibility.

By identifying the capabilities you need, exploring different
resourcing options, and focusing on hiring and retaining the right
people, you'll be well on your way to building your dream team
and achieving your business goals.

Technology plays a crucial role in how your team delivers
client services, providing efficiencies, cost savings and increased
client engagement. The next chapter will explore how to leverage
technology to optimise your business operations.

CHAPTER 19

DELIVER EXCEPTIONAL CLIENT SERVICES: BUILDING TRUST AND ACHIEVING RESULTS

Delivering exceptional client services is the cornerstone of any successful consulting business. In my years at Harrisons, I've learned that effective service delivery requires more than just completing the task at hand; it demands a deliberate focus on building trust, setting clear expectations and maintaining open communication. In this chapter, we'll explore how to scope, plan, execute and review client services, ensuring your work consistently exceeds expectations. I'll also share insights from Harrisons to illustrate how a structured approach can make a real difference.

BUILDING TRUST THROUGH CREDIBILITY AND COMMUNICATION

One of the first lessons I learned was the importance of trust in client relationships. Trust doesn't happen by accident; it is built on a foundation of credibility and effective communication. At Harrisons, we use a model for influence that starts with credibility. To establish credibility, you must focus on discovery – asking the right questions and truly listening to understand the client's needs. This isn't just about their business goals but also about personal drivers and pain points.

Once you've established a clear understanding of their needs, you bring in your knowledge and expertise. Credibility grows when you can demonstrate your understanding through well-researched insights, a strong business case and the application of your skills to solve their challenges. Your actions – delivering on time, maintaining commercial focus and clear project management – reinforce this credibility. As you deliver measurable results, backed by metrics and thoughtful communication of outcomes, you cement trust. With trust established, you gain influence, enabling you to help clients implement meaningful changes.

THE HR BUSINESS PARTNERING APPROACH

A fundamental shift in the HR profession over the past few decades has been the move from a purely administrative function to a strategic business partner model, pioneered by HR legend, Dave Ulrich. His HR Business Partner (HRBP) model focuses on aligning HR practices with business goals, ensuring that HR plays a proactive and value-adding role in organisational success.

For HR consultants, adopting an HR business partnering approach is essential to building credibility and delivering impactful services. The model emphasises four key roles that HR professionals must play, with an ideal time allocation to ensure effectiveness:

1. **Strategic partner (30-40%)** – aligning HR strategy with business goals, ensuring that people practices drive organisational success. This includes workforce planning, organisational design and leadership capability building.
2. **Change agent (20-30%)** – leading transformation and supporting organisations through cultural and structural shifts. Consultants help businesses navigate change by ensuring leadership buy-in, employee adoption and communication strategies.
3. **Employee champion (20-30%)** – advocating for employees, improving engagement and fostering a positive workplace

culture. This includes coaching managers on leadership, conducting engagement surveys and implementing wellbeing initiatives.

4. **Administrative expert (10-20%)** – ensuring compliance, efficiency and operational excellence in HR processes. While essential, administrative tasks should be streamlined and automated where possible to free up time for higher-value work.

WHY BUSINESS PARTNERING MATTERS FOR HR CONSULTANTS

As consultants, we're not just external service providers – we need to act as true business partners, embedding ourselves in our clients' operations and helping leaders navigate complex workforce challenges. This means:

- taking the time to understand the business strategy and aligning HR solutions accordingly
- coaching managers rather than just providing HR solutions – empowering them to own their people responsibilities
- bringing data-driven insights to demonstrate the commercial impact of HR initiatives
- partnering with leadership to solve business problems through people, not just applying generic HR solutions.

At Harrisons, we follow this business partnering approach to ensure our clients don't just get HR advice – they get strategic guidance that elevates their business performance. Whether it's workforce planning, leadership coaching or implementing new HR systems, we focus on collaboration, influence and results.

For any HR consultant looking to build long-term client relationships, this approach is critical. By positioning yourself as a trusted advisor, rather than a transactional HR service provider, you'll create deeper client impact and long-term success.

SCOPING SERVICES AND SETTING EXPECTATIONS

Scoping services effectively is the foundation of a successful client relationship. A comprehensive scope helps clarify deliverables, timelines and costs upfront, ensuring everyone is aligned.

Start by conducting a detailed discovery process, engaging in open conversations with the client to define their pain points, goals and expectations. From here, draft a clear project plan that outlines milestones, key deliverables, resource requirements and a timeline.

It's critical to be realistic and transparent during this stage. Overpromising can lead to disappointment, while under-scoping can result in scope creep and financial loss. Establishing expectations early – both in terms of outcomes and the client's role in the process – sets the stage for a productive partnership. Remember, your role is not to do the work for the client but to act as a business partner, empowering managers and leaders to take ownership of outcomes.

DELIVERING WITH EXCELLENCE

Once the project is underway, execution becomes paramount. This is where structured project management and regular communication shine. Start with a kick-off meeting to confirm expectations, clarify roles and agree on milestones. Regular check-ins, validation steps and client review meetings throughout the project ensure alignment and allow for adjustments if needed.

Your goal during delivery is to maintain focus on quality and timelines. Share drafts or preliminary work for feedback, encouraging the client to remain engaged and invested. This iterative approach not only ensures the final product meets their expectations but also strengthens their trust in your process. Effective delivery also includes documenting every step, which provides clarity and accountability for both parties.

HOW HARRISONS SERVICES CLIENTS

At Harrisons, we've developed a robust approach to client service delivery that begins with the initial inquiry. We start by scoping the project thoroughly, estimating hours and associated fees, and crafting a proposal with a detailed scope of services. Once the client signs on, we hold a kick-off meeting to align on expectations, deliverables, timelines and milestones.

During the project, we maintain open communication through regular check-ins and reviews, ensuring the client is always in the loop. We deliver drafts and seek feedback to validate that the work aligns with their vision. Once the project is complete, we conduct a post-project service review to identify lessons learned and areas for improvement. This structured process ensures not only a high-quality outcome but also a strengthened relationship with the client.

CONTINUOUS IMPROVEMENT THROUGH FEEDBACK AND REVIEW

Delivering exceptional service doesn't end when the project is complete. Soliciting client feedback and conducting a thorough review of each project are essential steps in improving your processes and outcomes. Schedule a debrief with the client to discuss what went well, what could be improved and how they felt about the overall experience. This not only helps you refine your approach but also shows the client that you're committed to continuous improvement.

Measuring success is equally important. Establish clear metrics to evaluate whether the project achieved its objectives, whether it was delivered on time and within budget, and how satisfied the client was with the outcome. Use these insights to adapt your approach for future projects, ensuring you consistently meet and exceed client expectations.

CHECKLIST – DELIVERING EXCEPTIONAL CLIENT SERVICES

Use this checklist to ensure every client project is delivered with professionalism, clarity and measurable success.

Conduct a thorough discovery process
- Engage in meaningful conversations to uncover the client's goals, challenges and pain points.
- Use open-ended questions and active listening to establish a deep understanding of their needs.
- Document insights from the discovery phase to form the foundation of your service delivery.

Scope and define the project clearly
- Develop a detailed scope of work, including deliverables, timelines, milestones and responsibilities.
- Estimate hours and fees accurately, incorporating potential contingencies for scope changes.
- Present a well-structured proposal to align expectations and gain client buy-in.

Establish key expectations at a kick-off meeting
- Schedule a formal project initiation meeting to align with key stakeholders.
- Confirm agreed milestones, deliverables, resources and timelines.
- Discuss preferred communication methods, frequency of updates and escalation processes.

Build credibility and trust through delivery
- Demonstrate expertise by backing your recommendations with research, case studies or industry benchmarks.
- Maintain transparency and integrity in all communications to foster trust.
- Balance technical competence with empathy and understanding of client challenges.

Focus on regular client communication
- Schedule consistent check-ins and progress updates to ensure alignment.
- Share drafts or interim deliverables for feedback and validation at each stage.
- Be proactive in flagging potential issues or risks and discussing solutions collaboratively.

Deliver high-quality work with a client-focused approach
- Ensure deliverables meet or exceed agreed standards and are tailored to the client's needs.
- Validate outcomes with the client at every milestone to avoid surprises at the end.
- Strive to exceed expectations in both service delivery and professionalism.

Monitor and manage project hours and costs
- Regularly track time spent and costs against the project budget.
- Use project management tools or systems to monitor resource allocation.
- Flag potential overruns early and discuss rescoping or additional resources with the client as needed.

Conduct a post-project review
- Hold a formal review with the client to evaluate project outcomes and gather feedback.
- Reflect on what went well and identify areas for improvement for future projects.
- Document client testimonials or success stories to support marketing efforts.

Adopt a business partnering approach
- Collaborate with clients to empower their managers and teams rather than doing the work for them.
- Share tools, templates and processes to equip clients to sustain results independently.
- Use a consultative style to position yourself as a trusted advisor rather than just a service provider.

Measure and communicate results

- Identify and track relevant success metrics, such as process improvements, employee engagement or cost savings.
- Present results in a clear and impactful way, using reports, visual dashboards or presentations.
- Reinforce the value delivered by your services to strengthen the client relationship and foster long-term collaboration.

By following these principles and practices, you can deliver exceptional client services that build trust, establish influence and drive measurable results. This client-centric approach not only ensures successful projects but also fosters long-term relationships that support the growth and sustainability of your consulting business.

By streamlining your client service delivery with clear processes, effective communication and a focus on measurable results, you lay the foundation for exceptional client relationships and successful outcomes. In the next chapter, we'll explore how leveraging technology can further enhance your efficiency, helping you work smarter, not harder, while delivering even greater value to your clients.

CHAPTER 20

WORK SMARTER NOT HARDER, WITH TECH

In the fast-paced world of HR consulting, one of the smartest moves you can make is to leverage technology to streamline your operations and improve efficiency. Why spend hours manually doing tasks when there's an existing system that can do it for you – often better and faster?

By investing in the right technology, you'll free up valuable time to focus on what really matters: growing your business and delivering exceptional value to your clients. The abundance of affordable technology available today means that no matter the size of your consulting firm, there are tools to help you work smarter, not harder.

For HR consultants, technology is a game changer. Automation tools, CRM systems, project management software and other platforms can help you deliver client services more efficiently and effectively. By automating routine tasks, you'll not only save time but also reduce the risk of errors, streamline your processes and create a better overall experience for your clients.

WHY TECHNOLOGY IS CRITICAL FOR HR CONSULTANTS

As a consultant, your time is one of your most valuable assets. The more time you spend bogged down in administrative tasks, the less time you have to work on building your business or delivering value to your clients. Technology helps you work smarter by automating repetitive tasks, providing you with real-time data and insights and improving the efficiency of your day-to-day operations.

Here are some key reasons why technology is critical for HR consultants:

- **Increased efficiency** – automating tasks like client onboarding, invoicing and project management allows you to complete work faster and with fewer errors.
- **Scalability** – with the right tools in place, your business can scale more easily. Technology allows you to handle more clients and larger projects without increasing your workload.
- **Improved client experience** – streamlined processes and automation result in faster responses, more accurate information and a better overall experience for your clients.
- **Cost-effective** – investing in technology can save you money in the long run. By reducing the time spent on manual tasks, you can focus on higher-value work that generates revenue.

HOW HARRISONS USES TECH

At Harrisons, we've integrated a range of technology solutions to enhance both our internal processes and the client experience. Over the years, we've continuously sought out new tools and systems that help us deliver services more efficiently and free up time to focus on business growth. Of course, this is a work in progress – new technology becomes available all the time, and we're always evolving.

Here are some of the tools we currently use at Harrisons:

- **CRM for client onboarding** – our CRM (Customer Relationship Management) system is the backbone of our client onboarding process. It helps us track leads, automate follow-ups and manage all client communications in one place. This ensures that no lead falls through the cracks and clients have a smooth, professional onboarding experience.

- **Project management software** – we use project management software to handle everything from job costing to project timelines and invoicing. This tool helps us keep track of each project's progress, manage resources and ensure that all work is completed on time and within budget.
- **Subscriptions and automation for client compliance** – for many of our HR services, we've created automated templates for client compliance. These templates are subscription-based, allowing clients to access updated compliance documents automatically. This not only adds value to our clients but also generates recurring revenue for our business.
- **E-signing systems** – we use e-signature tools for everything from client proposals to employee onboarding documents. This saves time and makes the process easier for our clients, who can sign documents from anywhere, at any time.
- **Applicant Tracking System (ATS)** – recruitment is a service we offer, and our ATS helps us manage the hiring process for our clients. This tool allows us to track applicants, schedule interviews and streamline communication with both candidates and clients, making the recruitment process smoother and more efficient.

While we've made great strides in integrating technology, we recognise that it's an ever-evolving landscape. Staying open to new tools and innovations helps us maintain our competitive edge and continue delivering value to our clients.

STRATEGIES FOR WORKING SMARTER:
THE TECH TOOLS EVERY CONSULTANT NEEDS

If you're ready to start working smarter, not harder, there are four key strategies you can follow to implement the right technology for your business. Here's how you can start leveraging tech tools to improve efficiency and streamline your operations.

1. FUNCTION, JOB AND TASK ANALYSIS

The first step in adopting new technology is to analyse your current workflow. Take a close look at the tasks and functions within your business, and ask yourself:

- What are the tasks that take up the most time?
- Which tasks are repetitive and could be automated?
- Where are there bottlenecks in your processes that technology could help resolve?

By identifying these pain points, you'll have a clearer idea of which areas could benefit the most from automation or systemisation.

For example, if you find that client onboarding is taking up a lot of time, a CRM system could help streamline that process. If invoicing is cumbersome, accounting software with automated invoicing features could be a solution. The key is to identify where technology can have the greatest impact on your business.

HOW HARRISONS USES TECH

At Harrisons, one of our biggest challenges was managing information efficiently across multiple projects and clients. Initially, we relied heavily on spreadsheets for everything – document control, sales funnel tracking, job costing, time tracking and recruitment. While this worked in the early days, as the business grew, it became increasingly time-consuming and error-prone. We knew we needed a better system to streamline operations and free up time for higher-value work.

After researching options and consulting with IT specialists, we implemented Microsoft SharePoint for document control and sharing, which significantly improved collaboration and version management. We also introduced CRM software to automate marketing campaigns, track sales leads and manage client relationships more effectively. Project management, job costing and time-tracking software replaced our manual spreadsheets, making it easier to allocate resources and monitor profitability. For recruitment, we invested in specialist recruitment software, reducing admin time and improving candidate tracking.

Initially, adopting these new systems took time, and there was some resistance from the team. Learning new processes and moving away from familiar spreadsheets wasn't easy. However, once everyone saw the efficiency gains – faster access to information, automated reporting and fewer repetitive tasks – it became clear that the transition was well worth it. Now, we save countless hours on administrative work, allowing us to focus on delivering high-value client services.

2. SELECTING THE RIGHT SYSTEM

Once you've identified the areas where you need help, the next step is choosing the right technology. There are countless options available for every type of business function, so it's important to choose tools that align with your specific needs.

When evaluating different systems, consider the following:

- **Functionality** – does the tool have all the features you need to address your business challenges?
- **Ease of use** – is the system user-friendly, and will it be easy for you and your team to adopt?
- **Integration** – does the tool integrate with other systems you're already using (such as your CRM or project management software)?

- **Scalability** – will the system grow with your business, or will you outgrow it quickly?
- **Cost** – is the system cost-effective, considering the time and effort it will save you in the long run?

Research your options, read reviews and ask for demos where possible. Choosing the right system upfront will save you time and headaches down the road.

3. PROCESS MAPPING AND IDENTIFYING OPPORTUNITIES FOR IMPROVEMENT

Once you've selected the right systems, it's time to map out your processes. This involves documenting your current workflows and identifying areas where the new technology can be integrated to improve efficiency. Process mapping helps you see how tasks flow from one stage to the next and where there are opportunities to automate or streamline.

For example, if you're implementing a project management system, map out the entire project lifecycle – from the initial client meeting to final invoicing – and identify where the system can help automate tasks like scheduling, document sharing or invoicing.

This step is crucial for ensuring that you're using your new tools to their full potential and getting the maximum benefit from them.

4. IMPLEMENTING THE NEW TECHNOLOGY

After selecting and mapping out the new technology, the final step is **implementation**. This is where you'll roll out the new systems and ensure that everyone involved knows how to use them effectively.

Here's what to focus on during implementation:

- **Training** – provide comprehensive training for yourself and your team. Make sure everyone understands how to use the new system and how it fits into their daily workflow.
- **Documentation** – create procedures and guides that outline how the system should be used. This ensures consistency and makes it easier for new team members to get up to speed.

- **Monitoring** – after implementing the system, keep an eye on how it's performing. Are there any areas where it's not working as expected? Are there additional features you could be using? Monitoring the system's performance will help you make adjustments and get the most out of your investment.

CHECKLIST – TECH TOOLS FOR WORKING SMARTER – NOT HARDER

Here's a checklist to help you get started with integrating technology into your consulting business.

Task analysis
Review your daily and weekly tasks to identify repetitive, time-consuming, or manual processes that could be streamlined using technology.

System selection
Research and evaluate different technology options, considering functionality, ease of use, integration capabilities, scalability and cost-effectiveness.

Process mapping
Document your workflows to pinpoint inefficiencies and determine where automation or systemisation could enhance productivity and accuracy.

Implement automation tools
Identify opportunities to use automation tools for scheduling, invoicing, email follow-ups, data entry and other routine tasks.

Leverage a CRM system
Use a Customer Relationship Management (CRM) system to manage client interactions, track leads, automate follow-ups and streamline onboarding.

Adopt project management software
Integrate project management tools to improve team collaboration, track progress and ensure deadlines and budgets are met efficiently.

Enhance client experience with tech
Utilise e-signature tools, self-service portals and compliance automation to improve client interactions and service delivery.

Monitor system performance
Regularly review the effectiveness of your technology stack to ensure it aligns with your evolving business needs and makes daily operations more efficient.

Provide training and documentation
Ensure that you and your team understand how to use the new systems effectively by offering training and maintaining clear, accessible guides.

Continuously adapt and innovate
Stay updated on emerging technologies and trends, evaluating new tools that could further improve efficiency, scalability and client satisfaction.

Investing in technology is one of the smartest moves you can make as a consultant. By working smarter, not harder, you'll free up valuable time to focus on growing your business and delivering exceptional value to your clients. Whether it's a CRM system to manage leads, project management software to track progress or automation tools to streamline repetitive tasks, technology can help you scale your consulting business without burning out.

As you continue to grow, keep an eye on new tools and innovations that could further improve your efficiency. The world of technology is constantly evolving, and staying ahead of the curve will give you a competitive advantage and ensure that your business remains agile and ready for the future.

One life-changing technology that has become mainstream, making it readily accessible and affordable for small business owners, is Artificial Intelligence (AI) - the topic of the next chapter.

CHAPTER 21

THE FUTURE IS NOW: LEVERAGE AI

Artificial Intelligence (AI) is transforming the business landscape, enabling companies of all sizes to operate more efficiently, deliver exceptional value to clients and focus on high-impact strategic work. For small businesses and start-ups, AI offers an incredible opportunity to streamline processes, outsource non-core activities and improve productivity without significantly increasing costs. By using AI in strategic areas, consultants can save time, reduce repetitive tasks and focus on growing their business.

In this chapter, we'll explore the basics of AI, how it can be applied in small businesses, the latest trends in AI for HR, and some important ethical and legal considerations. I'll also share how we've embraced AI at Harrisons to enhance our operations, improve client service and drive growth. Finally, I'll provide practical recommendations for small consulting businesses looking to integrate AI and a checklist for getting started.

WHAT IS AI, AND HOW CAN SMALL BUSINESSES USE IT?

Artificial Intelligence (AI) refers to the development of computer systems that can perform tasks typically requiring human intelligence. This includes everything from natural language processing and image recognition to data analysis and decision-making. For HR consulting start-ups and small businesses, AI can automate repetitive tasks, provide data-driven insights and handle tasks that traditionally required more time and resources.

Here are some ways small HR businesses can leverage AI:

- **Marketing automation** – AI tools can automate social media posting, email marketing and lead nurturing sequences, ensuring consistent and targeted messaging across channels.
- **Content creation** – with AI-powered content tools, you can generate ideas, draft posts and even create entire articles, which can be a huge time-saver for busy consultants.
- **Client service** – AI chatbots are a cost-effective way to manage client inquiries, providing immediate responses and guiding potential clients through common questions.
- **Data analysis** – AI can quickly analyse large volumes of data, uncovering insights that can inform business strategy and help you understand your market better.
- **Sales and lead scoring** – AI algorithms can identify the most promising leads based on historical data, allowing you to prioritise high-quality leads and improve conversion rates.

For start-ups, leveraging AI in these areas means you can operate more efficiently without needing a large team. With the right AI tools, you can scale your business, improve client interactions and keep costs manageable.

THE FUTURE OF AI: TRENDS AND INNOVATIONS

AI is rapidly evolving, and it's changing the way businesses of all sizes approach operations, client service and growth. For small businesses, staying on top of AI trends can help maintain a competitive edge and ensure you're delivering modern, relevant services to clients. Some of the current trends in AI that are particularly relevant to your start-up HR consultancy include:

- **Natural Language Processing (NLP)** – NLP is enabling more conversational and accurate AI tools, like chatbots and virtual assistants, to manage client service inquiries. These systems can understand client queries better than ever and can handle more complex tasks, enhancing client satisfaction and freeing up people resources.

- **Predictive analytics** – AI-powered predictive analytics tools analyse historical data to forecast future trends, such as which marketing campaigns will perform best or which clients are likely to need specific services. This allows you to make data-driven decisions and optimise resources.

- **Personalisation** – AI can help personalise the client experience by analysing behaviour, preferences and past interactions. This allows you to offer tailored recommendations and targeted content, creating a more meaningful connection with each client.

- **Automation in HR** – in HR, AI is being used in many, many ways, including for applicant tracking, employee onboarding, performance management and employee sentiment analysis. These tools reduce administrative burdens and improve the efficiency of people-related processes.

While these trends offer exciting opportunities, it's essential to remember that AI is constantly evolving. By the time this book reaches your hands, there will be even more advancements, so staying open to new technologies and continuous learning will be key. I've attended seminars and industry events, including the Unleash World HR Tech and AI Conference in Paris, to gain insights from global experts and discover the latest innovations shaping the HR space. The team is highly engaged and curious, actively testing out the tools and resources introduced. We foster a culture of continuous learning, encouraging experimentation and discussion around AI-driven efficiencies that can enhance both our internal processes and client services.

AI TRENDS IN HR: WHAT'S EMERGING IN THE FIELD

AI is making a significant impact in the HR sector, helping to automate tasks and make data-driven decisions that benefit both consultants and their clients. Some specific trends in AI for HR consulting include:

- **Applicant tracking and recruitment automation** – AI-driven applicant tracking systems (ATS) can screen resumes, rank candidates and even conduct initial assessments, speeding up the recruitment process and helping HR consultants find the best fit for their clients more efficiently. Of note, AI is not by nature biased, but rather it's about the data being fed to the AI to make the hiring the decisions that may be biased. Be careful.

- **Employee sentiment analysis** – AI tools that analyse employee feedback, engagement surveys and other sentiment data can help consultants identify trends and address issues early on, improving the employee experience and reducing turnover.
- **Performance management** – AI can assist in monitoring employee performance and highlighting areas where additional training or support might be beneficial. Some tools use data from day-to-day tasks and communications to provide insights into employee productivity and engagement.
- **Compliance monitoring** – AI can support HR compliance by tracking changes in legislation and flagging any potential compliance risks within an organisation. This ensures that HR consultants can offer up-to-date guidance and avoid legal issues.

The integration of AI in HR is still a developing field, and as more tools become available, consultants can leverage these solutions to deliver better value, more efficiently. However, it's essential to keep in mind that AI solutions in HR should always be used ethically and responsibly.

ETHICAL AND LEGAL CONSIDERATIONS FOR USING AI

As beneficial as AI can be, it's important to consider the ethical and legal implications of using AI in business. Here are some considerations to keep in mind:

- **Data privacy** – AI systems often require significant amounts of data to function effectively. Ensure that any AI tools you use comply with data privacy laws, such as local regulations and the General Data Protection Regulation (GDPR), which is a regulation in the European Union (EU) that governs how personal data is collected, stored and used. Always handle client data responsibly, and be transparent about how you're using it.

- **Bias in AI** – AI algorithms can sometimes reflect biases present in their training data, which can lead to unfair or discriminatory outcomes. Be mindful of the potential for bias, especially when using AI tools for recruitment or performance evaluations.
- **Transparency** – Clients and employees should know when they're interacting with AI and understand how it's being used. Transparency builds trust and helps mitigate concerns about data use and privacy.
- **Accountability** – Ultimately, you are responsible for the actions of AI systems within your business. Ensure that AI decisions can be reviewed and that there's a human element in the decision-making process to address any errors or ethical concerns.

At Harrisons, we prioritise ethical AI use, focusing on tools that enhance our services and client experience without compromising data privacy, fairness or quality and relevance of advice. It's an area we constantly review as new guidelines and best practices emerge.

HOW HARRISONS USE AI

At Harrisons, we've embraced AI to streamline our operations, deliver a better client experience and improve our competitive edge. Here's how we use AI across different areas of our business:

- **Marketing and content development** – AI tools help us draft social media content, generate blog ideas and even create first drafts for certain types of content. This saves time and keeps our marketing consistent and relevant.
- **Lead nurturing** – Through AI-powered CRM systems, we can create personalised email sequences that engage leads based on their behaviour and interactions. These nurturing sequences keep our leads warm, even when they're not immediately ready to buy.

- **Proposals and tenders** – Drafting proposals and responding to tenders can be time-consuming. AI assists in automating parts of this process, ensuring that we're faster and more responsive in pitching to new clients.
- **Team communications** – AI-powered tools for communication and project management help our team collaborate more effectively, ensuring that everyone is aligned and informed, even in remote working set-ups.
- **Client service delivery** – AI enhances efficiency and accuracy in various consulting tasks, freeing up time for strategic client work. However, as qualified HR professionals, we are the experts – AI is a tool, not a substitute for professional judgment. We use AI to:
  - automate data entry, reporting and compliance checks to ensure accuracy and consistency, while always applying professional oversight
  - draft job advertisements, position descriptions and employee documents, which we then refine to ensure alignment with legal and client-specific needs
  - assist in structuring training workshop content and presentation materials, but we remain responsible for the quality, relevance and engagement of the final product
  - support the creation of organisational policies, procedures and contract clauses by providing draft content that we review and customise for each client's context
  - streamline proposal development by generating structured content, which we refine to ensure it accurately reflects client needs and business strategy
  - enhance webinar and online training delivery by assisting with scriptwriting and slide design, while we shape the final message and ensure it meets professional standards.

We continually explore, research and refine our AI usage to improve client outcomes, increase team efficiency, and stay ahead in a rapidly evolving business landscape – while always maintaining our role as trusted HR professionals who apply critical thinking, ethical considerations and human expertise to every aspect of our work.

PRACTICAL AI IDEAS FOR YOUR SOLO HR CONSULTING BUSINESS

If you're a solo consultant or a small start-up, here are five practical ways to start leveraging AI in your business:

1. **Automate repetitive tasks** – start with small, repetitive tasks like data entry, email responses or appointment scheduling. There are plenty of affordable AI tools available that can handle these tasks efficiently.

2. **Use AI for content generation** – AI tools can help generate content ideas, draft emails or create social media posts. This is a quick way to maintain an online presence without dedicating excessive time to content creation.

3. **Invest in an AI-powered CRM** – a CRM with AI capabilities can automate lead scoring, personalise email sequences and help manage client relationships. This will save you time and make your sales process more efficient.

4. **Explore chatbots for client service** – AI chatbots can handle initial client inquiries, providing quick responses and filtering leads. This ensures you only spend time on the most promising opportunities.

5. **Analyse data with AI** – many AI tools can analyse your website or social media data, helping you understand what's working and where to focus your efforts. This data-driven approach can guide your marketing and business development efforts.

CHECKLIST – GETTING STARTED WITH AI

Here's a checklist to help you get started with integrating AI into your consulting business.

Identify repetitive tasks
List time-consuming, repetitive tasks in your business that could be automated with AI, such as scheduling, invoicing or email responses.

Research AI tools
Explore available AI tools tailored to small businesses and HR consulting, considering affordability, ease of use and integration with existing systems.

Start with quick wins
Implement AI in simple areas first, such as automating emails, social media scheduling or client inquiries, to see immediate benefits without major investment.

Leverage AI for content creation
Use AI-powered writing tools to generate blog ideas, draft social media posts and streamline marketing content creation.

Adopt an AI-powered CRM
Invest in a CRM with AI capabilities to automate lead tracking, client follow-ups and personalised email sequences.

Enhance client experience with AI
Consider using AI-driven chatbots, automated responses or virtual assistants to improve client service and pre-qualify client inquiries.

Utilise AI for data-driven decision-making
Use AI analytics tools to track website engagement, social media interactions and marketing performance, gaining insights to optimise strategies.

Monitor AI performance and refine usage
Regularly assess the effectiveness of AI tools, measuring their impact on efficiency, client engagement and business outcomes.

Stay informed on AI advancements
Keep up with evolving AI trends, particularly in HR consulting
and business operations, to continually enhance your
competitive advantage.

Ensure ethical and responsible AI use
Review AI applications for potential biases, data privacy
concerns and transparency, ensuring compliance with ethical
and legal standards.

That concludes the Team section of my IGNITE framework, which is all about how you can resource your business to deliver products and services for profitable outcomes. As I've discussed, there are many flexible and affordable options to support your new and growing business.

I so wish I'd started my business with an increased level of resourcing and the benefit of AI. I should have hired my first person earlier. This would have enabled me to build my lifestyle business more quickly and with less sacrifice of time and money in the early days. Learn from my experience, and take action now to integrate smart resourcing and technology in your consulting business, so you can build success more efficiently and sustainably.

PART 6

EARN

PART 6 - EARN

For me, the numbers were always the easier part - I've always enjoyed them and had the background to manage budgets, cash flow and profitability. But early on, I learned that being good with numbers wasn't enough if the revenue wasn't coming in, or worse, if the work I was doing wasn't profitable. I was busy doing "things", but I wasn't focused enough on the right activities to generate revenue. I spent far too much time at networking events and giving presentations to people who weren't my target audience, or giving away free advice that didn't lead to paying clients. It wasn't until I received some great coaching that I realised I needed to get stricter with my time and more intentional about where I put my energy.

As the business grew, I faced another layer of complexity: ensuring profitability as I brought more people onto the team. That meant not only delivering great work but making sure it was done profitably. I got stricter about quoting, setting clear expectations with both clients and the team and monitoring every project to stay within budget. Implementing a job costing system was a game-changer for us, allowing us to track expenses, ensure we weren't over-delivering and keep profitability on track. Regular invoicing - preferably in advance - also helped us avoid the cash flow rollercoaster.

This section is about making your business work for you financially. Whether numbers come naturally to you or they feel like a necessary evil, mastering this area is critical. From getting your pricing right and managing costs to tracking profitability and invoicing on time, these chapters will give you practical tools to keep your business sustainable and successful. Profitability isn't just about working harder - it's about working smarter, staying focused and making sure your efforts pay off.

Earn is mastering your money to build a profitable business for your financial freedom.

CHAPTER 22

ESSENTIAL FINANCIAL PRACTICES FOR CONSULTANTS

Financial management may not be the most exciting part of running an HR consulting business, but it's absolutely essential to long-term success. In fact, sound financial practices are often what separates successful consultants from those who struggle. Whether you're a solo consultant or planning to build a team, understanding your financials gives you the power to make informed decisions, avoid cash flow issues and ensure your hard work translates into profitability.

For start-up consultants, getting the basics of financial management right from the beginning is crucial. This means not only knowing how much money is coming in and going out, but also being able to read and analyse your financial statements, plan for cash flow and budget for future expenses.

MY FINANCIAL MANAGEMENT JOURNEY
Financial management has been a priority for me from day one. Having a business degree with a minor in accounting (major in management) may have given me an advantage, but I wasn't immune to the learning curve of applying these principles when it came to my own business. I came very close to becoming an accountant, so I have a natural affinity for the discipline and structure financial management brings to a business. That said, even if

numbers aren't your thing, implementing basic financial practices is something every consultant can – and should – do.

One of the most important lessons I've learned is that you need to understand your costs, especially in a consulting business where time and other expenses can add up quickly. Knowing your expenses helps you price your services appropriately and ensure that each project is profitable. It's also essential to understand your profit and loss (P&L) statements, cash flow forecasts, and how your balance sheet reflects the health of your business. Yes, a good bookkeeper and accountant is important, but ultimately, the responsibility for understanding and managing your financials rests with you.

Managing the financials goes beyond simply tracking income and expenses. Weekly disciplines, such as invoicing clients promptly, making it easy for clients to pay and ensuring suppliers are paid on time, all contribute to financial health. It's essential to approach your finances with discipline and consistency. After all, we work incredibly hard to build our businesses, attract clients and deliver outstanding service – our financials should reflect that considerable effort.

ESSENTIAL FINANCIAL PRACTICES FOR START-UP CONSULTANTS

When you're running a start-up HR consulting business, there are specific financial practices you need to have in place. These five practices don't just ensure you stay afloat – they also set the stage for sustainable growth.

1. BUDGETING

Budgeting is one of the most basic, yet critical, financial practices. A budget allows you to plan your income and expenses over a certain period, helping you manage your cash flow and avoid unexpected shortfalls. For a consulting business, it's essential to budget for:

- **Recurring expenses** – office space hire/rent, utilities, software subscriptions, insurances and professional fees (for example, bookkeeper, accountant)

- **Variable expenses** – travel, venue hire, marketing, employee/ contractor/consultant fees and any other costs related to specific projects
- **Taxes** – setting aside a percentage of your income for taxes helps you avoid unpleasant surprises at tax time.

When creating a budget, be as realistic as possible and leave room for unforeseen expenses. A good rule of thumb is to budget conservatively on revenue and generously on expenses, so you're always prepared.

2. CASH FLOW MANAGEMENT

Cash flow is the lifeblood of any business. In consulting, it's easy to be caught off guard by cash flow issues, especially when clients take time to pay their invoices. Cash flow management involves tracking the money coming in to and going out of your business, ensuring you always have enough to cover expenses.

Here are some strategies to improve cash flow:

- **Invoice promptly** – send invoices immediately after completing a project or as per your agreed-upon terms. Or, better still, invoice fees in advance partly or fully. The sooner you invoice, the sooner you'll get paid.
- **Encourage prompt payments** – offer easy payment options like online payments, and consider incentives for early payments or penalties for late payments.
- **Set payment terms** – for larger projects, consider setting milestones and billing accordingly to maintain steady cash flow throughout the project lifecycle.
- **Create a cash reserve** – setting aside a portion of your income for emergencies can help you cover expenses during slow periods or unexpected shortfalls.

3. FINANCIAL REPORTING

Financial reports provide a snapshot of your business's health, allowing you to make informed decisions and identify any potential issues. At a minimum, it's important to understand and regularly review the following financial reports:

- **Profit and Loss Statement (P&L)** – shows your income, expenses and profit over a given period. It provides insight into your business's profitability and helps you track revenue trends.
- **Cash Flow Statement** – details cash inflows and outflows, giving you a real-time view of your liquidity. This is especially important for managing day-to-day expenses.
- **Balance Sheet** – lists your assets, liabilities and equity. It's an essential indicator of your business's financial stability and long-term viability.

Reviewing these reports monthly (at minimum) helps you spot any trends or red flags before they become major issues.

4. QUOTING AND PROJECT PROFITABILITY

In a consulting business, each project needs to be profitable on its own to ensure the overall health of the business. Understanding your costs is critical to quoting accurately and ensuring project profitability. When quoting, consider:

- **Direct costs** – any costs directly associated with the project, such as subcontractors, travel or specific software.
- **Indirect costs** – these include overhead expenses like rent, utilities, insurances and marketing that still impact project profitability.
- **Profit margin** – aim to build a profit margin into each project to ensure your business remains financially sustainable.

Tracking the actual costs versus your quoted price allows you to refine future quotes and identify areas where you may need to adjust pricing or reduce expenses.

5. INVOICING AND PAYMENT MANAGEMENT

Effective invoicing and payment management are essential for maintaining cash flow. Develop a system that makes it easy for clients to pay and ensures you get paid on time. Here are some invoicing best practices:

- **Use automated invoicing software** – many platforms allow you to create, send and track invoices automatically. This reduces errors and saves time.

- **Set clear payment terms** – clearly outline payment terms in your contracts, including due dates and late fees if applicable.
- **Follow up on overdue payments** – regularly check for overdue invoices and follow up with clients promptly. Consistent follow-ups show clients that you're serious about getting paid.

HEALTHY HABITS FOR FINANCIAL MANAGEMENT

As a consultant, adopting healthy financial habits will help you maintain control over your finances and make smart decisions as your business grows. Here are some key practices to integrate into your routine:

- **Review financials regularly** – set aside time each week to review your financial reports. This helps you stay aware of your current cash flow, outstanding invoices and upcoming expenses.
- **Plan for taxes** – taxes can be a major financial hit if you're not prepared. Set aside a percentage of your income each month to cover tax obligations, and work with a tax professional to ensure you're meeting all requirements.
- **Track expenses diligently** – use an expense tracking tool to record all business expenses. This will make it easier to claim deductions at tax time and understand your spending patterns.
- **Avoid debt when possible** – while business loans can be useful in certain cases, avoid relying on debt for day-to-day expenses. Aim to keep cash reserves for emergencies instead.

CHECKLIST – FINANCIAL MANAGEMENT

Here's a checklist to help you establish strong financial practices in your consulting business.

Weekly financial practices

- Issue invoices in advance: send invoices promptly to ensure a steady cash flow.
- Review and action billable/quoted hours: ensure all work is correctly logged and billed.
- Monitor cash flow and outstanding invoices: regularly track incoming payments and flag overdue invoices for follow-up.
- Track expenses and file receipts: keep digital records of expenses for accurate reporting and tax deductions.
- Follow up on overdue invoices: implement a structured follow-up process to ensure timely payments.

Monthly financial practices

- Review financial reports: analyse your Profit and Loss (P&L), cash flow statement and balance sheet to track financial health.
- Reconcile bank accounts: ensure all transactions are recorded correctly and match your business accounts.
- Set aside income for taxes: allocate a percentage of revenue to tax obligations to prevent financial stress.

Quarterly financial practices

- Assess project profitability: review costs vs revenue for completed projects and refine pricing strategies.
- Conduct a financial health check: evaluate cash flow trends, debt levels and operational efficiency.
- Meet with your accountant or bookkeeper: gain insights on financial performance and tax planning.
- Adjust financial goals and budgets: make data-driven updates to revenue targets, cost projections and investment plans.

Annual financial practices

- Set a financial plan for the new year: define revenue targets, pricing strategies and profitability goals.
- Adjust pricing and fee structures: ensure pricing reflects market trends, business growth and service value.
- Review and optimise expenses: identify opportunities to reduce unnecessary costs while maintaining service quality.
- Complete a tax strategy review: work with an accountant to minimise tax liabilities and plan for deductions.
- Assess financial technology tools: evaluate whether your accounting and financial tracking systems are still the best fit for your business.

Sound financial practices are the foundation of any successful consulting business. By taking control of your finances and establishing routines around budgeting, cash flow management and financial reporting, you'll set your business up for long-term success. While working with a bookkeeper or accountant is essential, the responsibility for understanding and managing your financials ultimately rests with you. Adopting healthy financial habits and regularly reviewing your financials will empower you to make strategic decisions and ensure your business remains profitable and sustainable.

Critical to your business's financial success is how you decide to profitably price your services, which I will cover in the next chapter.

CHAPTER 23

PROFITABLE PRICING: VALUE YOUR VALUE

One of the most critical aspects of running a successful consulting business is ensuring that your pricing not only covers costs but also generates profit. I've seen many consultants struggle with pricing, often undercharging out of fear of losing clients or a reluctance to value their expertise appropriately. Unfortunately, incorrect pricing can lead to not enough revenue, cash flow issues and a frustrating sense of financial instability. I've even seen consultants feel so desperate to return to the "steady income" of being an employee that they end up abandoning their entrepreneurial dreams altogether.

The truth is, pricing your consulting services isn't just about numbers; it's about valuing yourself – your time, experience and the unique benefits you bring to clients. In this chapter, we'll discuss the downsides of getting pricing wrong, why it's essential to value yourself and your services and how to develop a pricing strategy that sustains your business.

THE IMPORTANCE OF PRICING YOUR CONSULTING SERVICES CORRECTLY

Pricing can make or break a consulting business. Set your prices too low, and you'll struggle with cash flow, constantly worrying about paying bills and wondering why you're not saving enough. Worse, you may even find it challenging to pay yourself a reasonable salary. On the other hand, set your prices too high without a clear justification and you may struggle to attract clients, especially if they don't understand the value you bring.

Getting pricing right means:

- **Ensuring steady revenue** – with the right pricing, you can maintain a consistent cash flow, ensuring that bills are paid, savings are built and you're adequately compensated.

- **Packaging services** – in the earlier Niche section we discussed the importance and benefits of packaging and productising your services, and/or offering a subscription type service.

- **Reflecting your value** – clients aren't just paying for your time; they're paying for your years of experience, knowledge and the positive impact you bring to their business using that expertise.

- **Sustaining your business** – profitability isn't just about covering immediate costs. It's about building a financially sustainable business that allows you to save, invest in growth and ride out the natural ups and downs.

Understanding and valuing the impact you have on clients is crucial. Consulting fees should reflect your expertise, not just the hours you spend with a client. When you've dedicated years to building knowledge and skills, you've earned the right to be fairly compensated for the value you provide.

MY JOURNEY TO PROFITABLE PRICING

When I first started, I undervalued my time and expertise. Although I had a background in HR, with studies in business and accounting, I still struggled with pricing because, like many, I worried about pricing myself out of opportunities. However, I soon realised that undervaluing my services – and time – led to more issues than it solved. I had less cash flow, found myself stressed about finances and felt underappreciated for the hard work I was putting in. I seriously considered packing it up and going back to a corporate job.

Over time, a major turning point for me was realising that I was earning a quarter of what I had made in my corporate role while working just as much. I was giving away too much free time, undercharging, and justifying it by thinking I had to prove my worth to clients. But then it hit me – I was solving major, expensive problems for businesses using my significant experience and knowledge, and I deserved to be paid accordingly. If I didn't shift my mindset and pricing, I knew I'd be forced back into corporate life, and I REALLY didn't want that. That was my wake-up call.

For those who don't have 30 years of experience, don't let that hold you back. You don't need decades in the field to be highly valuable – what matters is that you are solving real problems for your clients, and that is worth a lot. Instead of focusing on years of experience, focus on the outcomes you deliver, the headaches you remove and the confidence you give your clients. The value isn't just in how long you've worked in HR – it's in how well you help your clients achieve their goals.

Another essential lesson I've learned is to account for all business costs when setting prices. My pricing includes not just my time but also all operational expenses, including the cost of employees, systems, office, insurances, tax and our team celebrations. It's important to remember that you're building a business, not just trading hours for income. By setting profitable prices, we now maintain a steady cash flow and savings in the business, ensuring that paying the bills is never an issue and that I can pay myself a good salary with benefits.

THE CONSEQUENCES OF POOR PRICING

When pricing is set too low, it can lead to a cascade of financial and operational problems. Here are some of the downsides I've seen in businesses where pricing doesn't reflect the true value of services:

1. **Cash flow problems** – insufficient cash flow can lead to difficulty paying bills, which then puts stress on the business owner. This pressure can hinder growth, as financial insecurity prevents you from making strategic investments.
2. **Inability to save** – without a healthy profit margin, saving for business growth or emergencies becomes challenging, leaving the business vulnerable to unexpected downturns.
3. **Low earnings** – if your pricing doesn't support both the business and your income, you may end up earning less than

you would as an employee. This can lead to frustration, financial stress and burnout.

4. **Desperation to revert to employment** – for some consultants, poor pricing leads to a lack of financial stability, which can eventually cause them to give up on consulting and return to employment. Pricing appropriately is essential to maintaining a financially viable and fulfilling consulting career.

HOW TO SET PROFITABLE PRICES IN YOUR CONSULTING BUSINESS

Now that we've established why pricing is so critical, let's look at the five practical steps you can take to set profitable prices in your HR consulting business. The key is to develop a pricing strategy that accounts for all costs, values your expertise and ensures a healthy profit margin.

1. UNDERSTAND YOUR COSTS

Begin by calculating all the costs associated with running your business. These include:

- **Direct costs** – expenses that relate directly to delivering services, like software, materials, travel or subcontractors.
- **Overheads** – ongoing expenses such as rent, utilities, insurance, marketing and professional fees.
- **Team costs** – if you have employees or contractors, include their salaries, benefits and any related taxes.

Understanding these costs is essential for pricing each service line profitably. Once you know your total costs, you can calculate how much revenue you need to cover them.

2. VALUE YOUR EXPERTISE AND EXPERIENCE

One of the most challenging aspects of pricing is recognising and valuing your expertise. Clients aren't just paying for your time – they're paying for your unique skills, experience, and the years you've invested in honing your craft. Consider what your advice, strategies and solutions are worth to the client.

If your pricing feels high when converted to an hourly rate, remember that clients aren't just paying for the hour you spend with them. They're paying for the years of expertise, industry knowledge and innovative practices that enable you to provide such high value. This perspective shift can help you set pricing that truly reflects the value you bring.

3. INCLUDE A PROFIT MARGIN

In addition to covering costs, your prices should include a profit margin that allows your business to grow, save and reinvest in areas like marketing, training or new technology. Profitability isn't a bonus; it's a necessity. Aim to build a profit margin into each project or service to ensure your business remains financially sustainable.

Profitability allows you to:
- save for future investments or expansion
- build a financial buffer for slow periods
- compensate yourself fairly, reducing stress and improving work satisfaction.

4. RESEARCH INDUSTRY STANDARDS

It's also helpful to research what similar consulting businesses are charging. Understanding industry standards provides a benchmark and ensures your pricing is competitive. However, don't set prices solely based on competitors – ensure your rates also reflect your costs, expertise and the unique value you offer.

5. OFFER VALUE-BASED PRICING

For certain consulting services, consider value-based pricing. This approach charges based on the perceived value to the client rather than the time spent. For example, if a service helps a client increase their employee retention, the value to them might be significant enough to justify a higher price. Value-based pricing focuses on results, allowing you to charge more for services that deliver measurable impact.

CHECKLIST - PROFITABLE PRICING

To help you establish profitable pricing in your consulting business, here's a checklist of key steps.

Calculate costs

- Identify direct costs (software, materials, travel, subcontractors).
- Account for overheads (rent, utilities, insurance, marketing, professional fees).
- Include team costs (employees, contractors, benefits, payroll taxes).
- Determine the minimum revenue needed to cover costs and ensure profitability.

Value your expertise and experience

- Recognise that clients pay for your knowledge, not just your time.
- Factor in the years of experience, industry insights and problem-solving ability.
- Adjust pricing to reflect specialised skills or unique methodologies.
- Shift your mindset from hourly rates to outcomes and results.

Set a sustainable profit margin

- Ensure prices exceed costs to maintain a profitable business.
- Build in a profit buffer to save, reinvest and handle slow periods.
- Use margin-based pricing rather than undercutting competitors.
- Consider long-term financial goals when determining profit percentage.

Research competitor pricing and market standards

- Compare your rates to industry benchmarks for similar services.
- Identify premium pricing opportunities based on niche expertise.
- Avoid the trap of low pricing just to win clients - value and results matter.
- Ensure your pricing reflects both competitive rates and your unique positioning.

Consider value-based pricing

- Identify services where pricing can be outcome-driven rather than time-based.
- Communicate the ROI (Return on Investment) clients get from your services.
- Package services for greater perceived value rather than charging by the hour.
- Offer tiered pricing models to cater to different client budgets and needs.

Develop confidence in your pricing strategy

- Own your value – don't feel guilty about charging appropriately.
- Understand that discounting lowers perceived value of your expertise.
- Be prepared to educate clients on the benefits of your pricing model.
- Adjust pricing annually based on market trends and business growth.

Setting profitable prices isn't just about numbers; it's about valuing yourself and the work you do. Clients come to you because they need your expertise, guidance and solutions – and that's worth paying for. By setting prices that reflect your value, cover costs and include a healthy profit margin, you'll create a financially sustainable business that allows you to grow, save and continue delivering exceptional value to clients.

The most important lesson in pricing is to remember that you're building a business, not just trading hours for income. Profitable pricing not only ensures you can cover expenses but also enables you to build a consulting business that provides the financial stability, rewards and satisfaction that make the entrepreneurial journey worthwhile.

In the next chapter, we'll dive into tracking your financials to ensure you're staying profitable and in control of your business finances.

CHAPTER 24

KNOW YOUR NUMBERS: INCOME AND EXPENSES

In the world of consulting, it's not only about bringing in revenue – it's also about **controlling costs**. Good cost management ensures that every dollar earned works towards building a sustainable, profitable business. For consultants, who often have both fixed and variable expenses, cost control can make a huge difference to profitability. Without careful oversight, costs can quickly spiral, eroding profits and creating cash flow challenges. Effective cost management helps you maintain financial stability, weather unexpected changes and ultimately keep profits high.

In this chapter, we'll explore strategies for monitoring and controlling business expenses, with insights on budgeting, fore-casting and handling larger expenses. I'll also share my approach to cost management at Harrisons, including practical tips to keep spending under control without compromising quality. Finally, we'll go over a checklist to help you put these practices into action.

THE COST OF POOR MANAGEMENT: AVOIDING PITFALLS

Avoiding good cost management can be risky. Without proper control over expenses, even a profitable consulting business can struggle financially. Poor cost management often leads to:

- **Cash flow problems** – uncontrolled spending can strain cash flow, especially in months with lower revenue. This can make it difficult to pay bills, suppliers or even yourself.
- **Debt accumulation** – when expenses aren't well-managed, it's easy to fall into a cycle of debt, using loans or credit to cover shortfalls rather than addressing the root cause of overspending.
- **Reduced profit margin** – high expenses reduce profitability, even if revenue is strong. Without a healthy profit margin, it's challenging to save for growth, emergencies or future investments.

For consultants, the solution lies in proactive and thoughtful management of expenses, building habits and systems that keep costs low and profits high.

KEY STEPS FOR GOOD COST MANAGEMENT

Effective cost management involves a combination of careful planning, regular monitoring and smart financial decisions. Here's an eight-step approach to managing costs in a way that supports profitability and financial stability.

1. SET A BUDGET

A budget is the foundation of good cost management. It allows you to plan your expenses based on anticipated revenue, ensuring you don't overspend or allocate funds ineffectively. For consultants, budgeting should include:

- **Fixed costs** – these are expenses you incur regardless of revenue, such as rent, insurance, software subscriptions and internet services.
- **Variable costs** – these expenses fluctuate based on project needs or revenue levels, including subcontractor fees, travel or marketing.

Review your budget regularly to ensure that it aligns with your actual spending and revenue. If you have a particularly lean month, consider adjusting your budget to maintain positive cash flow.

2. MONITOR AND TRACK SPENDING

A budget is only as effective as your ability to stick to it. Tracking expenses consistently helps you stay on top of where your money is going and quickly address any areas of overspending.

There are various tools available for expense tracking, from accounting software to simple spreadsheets. The important thing is to review your expenses regularly, ideally on a weekly or monthly basis, to identify trends, make adjustments and avoid surprises.

3. USE SEPARATE ACCOUNTS FOR TAXES AND SAVINGS

One of the simplest ways to manage cash flow and avoid financial stress is to set aside funds for taxes, longer-term expenses and emergencies in separate accounts. By earmarking funds for specific purposes, you reduce the temptation to spend them and ensure that you're financially prepared for tax season or unexpected expenses.

For example, at Harrisons, we have separate accounts for:

- **Taxes** – a portion of revenue is set aside in a dedicated account to cover quarterly or annual tax payments.
- **Long-term expenses** – funds for larger expenses, such as software upgrades, professional development or equipment, are saved gradually in this account.
- **Emergency savings** – this is a "rainy day" fund to help manage unexpected costs, such as a sudden drop in revenue or an unplanned expense.

These accounts not only improve financial discipline but also provide peace of mind, knowing that you're prepared for both expected and unexpected costs.

4. FORECAST CASH FLOW

Cash flow forecasting is a crucial practice that helps you predict your financial position over a specific period, usually on a monthly or quarterly basis. A cash flow forecast takes into account both expected revenue and upcoming expenses, allowing you to plan for periods of lower revenue or higher costs.

To create a cash flow forecast:

- **Estimate monthly revenue** – use historical data or anticipated project income to project future revenue.
- **Identify fixed and variable costs** – list all known expenses and estimate any variable costs based on past trends or planned activities.
- **Adjust for seasonality** – if your consulting business has peak and slow periods, factor these fluctuations into your forecast.

At Harrisons, cash flow forecasting is a key part of our financial planning. By understanding our cash flow, we can make informed decisions about larger investments, marketing expenses or team expansion.

5. TAKE ADVANTAGE OF DISCOUNTS AND PAYMENT TERMS

Sometimes, small savings add up significantly over time. Look for opportunities to take advantage of discounts, early payment incentives or flexible payment terms. Many suppliers and vendors offer discounts if you pay in advance or within a certain time-frame. If this option is available, consider using it to save on recurring expenses.

For example, some software providers or membership organisations offer annual payment discounts. By opting to pay annually rather than monthly, you can reduce costs without compromising the services or benefits you need.

6. MANAGE LARGER EXPENSES WISELY

Larger expenses, like taxes or insurance premiums, can put a strain on cash flow if not managed effectively. If you're just starting out or cash flow is tight, consider using instalment plans to spread out these costs over time. This approach allows you to handle necessary expenses without draining your cash reserves all at once.

When I started Harrisons, instalment plans were invaluable in helping us manage significant expenses while keeping cash flow steady. Whether it's taxes, insurance or software purchases, spreading costs over time can relieve financial pressure and keep the business running smoothly.

7. FOCUS ON KEY FINANCIAL INDICATORS

Tracking a few core financial indicators can provide valuable insights into the health of your business. Some indicators to monitor include:

- **Job profitability** – track profitability by project or client to ensure each job contributes positively to your bottom line.
- **Billable hours** – keep track of billable hours versus non-billable hours to understand how much time is spent on revenue-generating activities.
- **New business and client acquisition** – monitoring the number of new clients or projects helps you understand whether your business is maintaining, decreasing or growing, and therefore what to expect in the way of income.
- **Aging of accounts receivable** – track overdue invoices and follow up regularly to keep cash flow healthy.

These indicators offer a snapshot of your financial position, making it easier to adjust pricing, identify cost-saving opportunities or address slow-paying clients.

8. OFFER RECURRING OR SUBSCRIPTION SERVICES

As mentioned in previous chapters, offering recurring or subscription-based services is a great way to smooth out income and improve cash flow. Monthly retainers or subscription services not only provide clients with a consistent level of support but also help your business maintain a predictable revenue stream. This approach can make budgeting and cash flow management significantly easier.

HOW HARRISONS MANAGE COSTS

There's nothing worse than when the big tax bill arrives and you don't have the money to pay it (I'm optimistic you'll make enough money to have a big tax bill!) This happened to me several times in the early years. Fortunately, the tax office provided a payment plan but that comes at a cost.

This is one of those times when you need the Growth Mindset we covered earlier in the Inspire section.

At Harrisons, cost management has always been a priority. We set budgets for various areas of the business, including revenue by service area, operations, marketing and team, as well as professional development. Each budget is monitored closely, and any deviations are addressed immediately. Cash flow forecasting helps us anticipate leaner months and adjust expenses accordingly.

We also set up separate savings accounts for taxes, long-term expenses and emergencies, ensuring that we're always prepared for both expected and unexpected costs. By taking advantage of early payment discounts, using instalment plans for larger expenses and focusing on key financial indicators, we've created a financial foundation that supports both stability and growth. Sometimes I have also paid expenses in weekly payments in advance just to help me with my cashflow and ensure that the larger expenses were covered, for example those big tax bills.

One of the biggest lessons I've learned is the importance of accurately quoting for each project, including a buffer for any unforeseen expenses. This helps ensure that each job is profitable and that our pricing remains sustainable.

CHECKLIST – COST MANAGEMENT FOR CONSULTANTS

Here's a checklist to help you implement effective cost management practices.

Set a budget and review regularly
- Establish fixed and variable expense budgets for key areas like operations, marketing and professional development.
- Adjust budgets monthly to reflect actual revenue and costs.
- Maintain a conservative revenue forecast and a generous expense buffer to ensure financial stability.

Track and control spending
- Use accounting software or spreadsheets to monitor expenses weekly or monthly.
- Identify unnecessary expenses and reduce non-essential spending.
- Regularly review subscription costs and cancel or adjust underutilised services.

Separate accounts for taxes and savings
- Set up a dedicated tax savings account and deposit a percentage of revenue regularly.
- Maintain a long-term expense account for future investments (software, training, large expenses).
- Establish an emergency fund to cover unexpected financial gaps.

Forecast and manage cash flow
- Develop a monthly cash flow forecast to predict revenue and expenses.
- Identify peak and slow periods to adjust spending and revenue strategies accordingly.
- Use instalment payment plans for large expenses to smooth out cash flow.

Leverage payment terms and cost savings
- Take advantage of early payment discounts or negotiate flexible payment terms with vendors.
- Opt for annual payments instead of monthly subscriptions where possible to save costs.
- Automate weekly or bi-weekly pre-payments for large expenses to ease financial burden.

Monitor key financial indicators
- Track job profitability to ensure each project contributes positively to the bottom line.
- Measure billable vs non-billable hours to optimise productivity.
- Monitor new business and client acquisition rates to ensure revenue consistency.
- Stay on top of accounts receivable aging to minimise overdue payments.

Offer recurring revenue models
- Implement subscription-based or retainer services to stabilise cash flow.
- Structure client contracts with fixed-fee, ongoing service packages where applicable.

Implement smart cost management strategies
- Regularly review and adjust pricing models to reflect inflation and rising business costs.
- Use financial planning software to automate invoicing, budgeting and reporting.
- Conduct a quarterly financial health check to evaluate cost efficiency and profitability.

Cost management is one of the most important aspects of maintaining profitability and financial stability in a consulting business. By setting a budget, tracking expenses, forecasting cash flow and taking advantage of financial efficiencies, you can build a business that's financially resilient and prepared for growth. With disciplined cost management, you're not only ensuring profitability but also creating a foundation for a sustainable consulting business that thrives in the long term.

Financial management is only one piece of the puzzle when running a consulting business. To operate successfully and protect yourself from risk, it's essential to understand the legal and compliance obligations that come with running your own business. In the next chapter, we'll explore the key legal considerations for consultants, including contracts, liability protection and compliance requirements.

CHAPTER 25

UNDERSTAND AND COVER THE LEGALITIES OF BUSINESS

Running a professional services business means managing risk effectively to ensure sustainability, professionalism and legal compliance. Protecting your business starts with understanding your obligations and establishing clear terms with clients and team members. This chapter will guide you through the key aspects of risk mitigation, ensuring you operate with clarity and confidence.

THE HARD LESSON OF PROFESSIONAL INDEMNITY CLAIMS

For the first time in over 15 years of running my business, we faced a professional indemnity claim. It wasn't from a client but from the former employee of a client who had brought a claim against both her ex-employer and Harrisons. The allegation was that we had not supported her sufficiently during a workplace investigation.

By the time the matter reached mediation, it had already occurred a few years prior. Unfortunately, the Harrisons consultant who had conducted the investigation was no longer employed with us and had not maintained sufficient records to assist in our defence effectively. To further complicate the situation, our consultant had allegedly spoken with the claimant from her car while driving and therefore was perceived as not taking the matter seriously nor was she able to take notes of the conversation. This added to the difficulty in presenting a professional and well-documented defence. (Note – I completely agree that an investigation should not have been carried out from the consultant's vehicle and was appalled that this conduct was associated with Harrisons.)

Thankfully, we had Professional Indemnity insurance, which provided essential coverage during this stressful time. However, the situation still required significant effort, resources and time to defend, and impacted our insurance premium.

The experience taught us critical lessons about risk mitigation and professional practice standards, such as:

- **Supervise and support your team thoroughly** – ensure all consultants, especially those managing sensitive cases, are adequately supervised and supported.
- **Prioritise comprehensive record-keeping** – accurate and complete records are essential. Every conversation, decision and document related to client work should be meticulously documented.
- **Maintain professional communication standards** – all client-related conversations should be held in professional settings and documented appropriately. Avoid informal communication channels for sensitive matters.
- **Regular training and quality control** – implement ongoing training and quality control checks to ensure record-keeping and communication standards are consistently met.
- **Secure professional indemnity insurance** – while insurance provided critical protection, it should be viewed as a last line of defence. Proactive practices prevent claims in the first place.

This experience reinforced that professional accountability, proper supervision and strong systems are vital not just for compliance but for protecting the integrity of our business. It was a tough but invaluable lesson, and it's made us stronger as a team, with better processes to safeguard against similar issues in the future.

CLIENT TERMS AND CONDITIONS

One of the foundational steps in mitigating risk is setting clear and comprehensive client terms and conditions. Before beginning any work with a client, it is crucial to provide a formal document outlining:

- **Scope of services** – clearly detail what services you will provide, including deliverables, timelines and exclusions.
- **Fees and payment terms** – specify the fees, payment structure, timelines and consequences of late or non-payment.
- **Liabilities and limitations** – define your liability limitations, ensuring they align with your business model and industry standards.
- **Confidentiality and data protection** – include clauses about protecting client data and respecting privacy regulations.
- **Dispute resolution** – outline the steps to resolve disputes, including jurisdiction and governing law.

Ensure all terms are signed and agreed upon by both parties before commencing any work. A signed agreement reduces misunderstandings and provides a clear reference point should disputes arise.

LEGAL CONSIDERATIONS

Understanding and complying with legal obligations is essential for business stability and risk mitigation. Legal frameworks vary across countries, making it vital to:

- **Research local laws** – familiarise yourself with the business regulations in your operating regions.
- **Consult legal professionals** – engage with legal counsel to draft and review your standard agreements, contracts and business practices.
- **Intellectual property protection** – safeguard your intellectual property, including trademarks, copyrights and proprietary methodologies.
- **Data privacy compliance** – ensure your systems comply with data protection laws relevant to your market.

Staying legally compliant helps prevent fines, lawsuits and reputational damage while fostering trust with clients.

BUSINESS INSURANCES

Insurance plays a critical role in protecting your business from unexpected financial risks. Essential business insurances include:

- **Professional indemnity insurance** – protects against claims of professional negligence, errors or omissions.
- **Public liability insurance** – covers claims related to injury or property damage occurring in connection with your business activities.
- **Workers' compensation** – required in many countries to cover employee injuries sustained at work.
- **Property insurance** – protects business premises, equipment and physical assets.

Work with a qualified insurance broker to ensure you meet legal requirements and choose the right coverage for your industry and business size.

EMPLOYMENT CONTRACTS

Whether you employ people directly, offshore roles, use virtual assistants (VAs) or hire contractors, clear and compliant employment agreements are essential. These agreements should cover:

- **Terms of engagement** – clarify whether the engagement is permanent, temporary, contract-based or freelance.
- **Duties and responsibilities** – clearly outline job expectations and performance standards.
- **Remuneration and benefits** – specify payment terms, including wages, bonuses and benefits.
- **Confidentiality and non-compete** – address protection of business information and competitive practices.
- **Termination clauses** – detail the notice period and grounds for termination.

Work with legal professionals to ensure your contracts comply with the employment laws in your operating regions.

THE IMPORTANCE OF RECORD-KEEPING

Good record-keeping is fundamental to effective risk management. Ensure you:

- maintain digital and physical records of all contracts, agreements and signed documents
- keep records of communications with clients and team members, especially regarding agreements and disputes
- store insurance policies, employment agreements and compliance certifications in a secure location
- use a document management system to track renewals, contract end dates and policy expirations.

CHECKLIST – RISK MITIGATION FOR CONSULTANTS

Use this checklist to help you stay on top of your risk management and compliance obligations.

Establish clear client agreements
- Provide detailed terms and conditions outlining scope, fees, timelines and liability.
- Include confidentiality and data protection clauses to safeguard client information.
- Define a dispute resolution process to manage conflicts professionally.
- Ensure contracts are signed before work commences to avoid misunderstandings.

Ensure legal compliance
- Research local business regulations to stay compliant with relevant laws.
- Work with legal advisors to review contracts and policies.
- Protect intellectual property with trademarks, copyrights or proprietary clauses.
- Implement data privacy and cybersecurity measures in line with applicable laws.

Secure business insurance
- Obtain Professional Indemnity Insurance to cover claims of professional negligence.
- Get Public Liability Insurance to protect against third-party injury or property damage.
- Ensure Workers' Compensation Insurance is in place for employees.
- Review Property and Cyber Insurance for office equipment, digital assets and online risks.

Draft and maintain employment contracts
- Clearly outline terms of engagement for employees, contractors, offshore staff or VAs.
- Define job roles, responsibilities and performance expectations.
- Specify payment terms, benefits and leave entitlements.
- Include confidentiality, intellectual property and non-compete clauses.
- Detail termination terms to avoid disputes and legal risks.

Prioritise accurate record-keeping
- Maintain secure digital and physical copies of contracts, policies and agreements.
- Document client communications, key project milestones and any disputes.
- Store insurance certificates, employment agreements and regulatory compliance documents in an accessible, secure location.
- Use document management software to track contract renewal dates and policy expirations.

Ongoing legal and compliance reviews
- Regularly review and update contracts, policies and agreements to align with legal changes.
- Conduct annual risk assessments to identify and mitigate potential business liabilities.
- Stay informed on industry standards, employment law updates and regulatory changes.
- Provide legal and risk training for yourself and your team to reinforce best practices.

Proactively managing risk and legal compliance isn't just about protecting your business – it's about setting a strong foundation for long-term success. With clear agreements, proper insurance and effective record-keeping, you minimise disputes, enhance professionalism and operate with confidence.

In the next section, we'll bring together everything from the IGNITE framework to create a structured, actionable plan that transforms your consulting business into a sustainable, profitable venture.

YOUR PLAN
TO IGNITE

YOUR PLAN TO IGNITE

You've reached the final section of my book, and I want to take a moment to acknowledge the journey you've just completed. You've explored IGNITE, my personal framework for building and sustaining a successful HR consulting firm. I hope this book has not only shared valuable insights but also given you practical tools to help you build a thriving business, just as I have done with my own HR consulting journey.

The lessons and strategies I've shared come from real experiences – the successes, the setbacks and everything in between. This book represents more than just concepts; it's my story, shaped by years of navigating the challenges and triumphs of building a business I am proud of. I hope it has been as empowering and insightful for you as it was for me to write it.

Looking back, there are so many things I wish I'd known when I first started. I wish I had truly understood the value of my time and expertise – that I didn't need to say yes to every opportunity or underprice my services to attract clients. I wish I had invested in systems and processes earlier, rather than trying to juggle everything myself. And perhaps most importantly, I wish I had trusted myself more – that I had the skills, knowledge and experience to build a thriving business without second-guessing every decision.

But every challenge, mistake and lesson along the way has shaped the business I have today. That's why I wrote this book – to give you the insights, shortcuts and confidence I wish I had when I started. You don't have to figure it all out the hard way. With clarity, persistence and the right approach, you can fast-track your success and build an HR consulting business that truly works for you.

Now, as you turn these final pages, the focus shifts from learning to doing. It's time to take the knowledge you've gained and turn it into meaningful action. Whether you're just starting your HR consulting business or have already taken the leap into self-employment but feel like you're struggling to gain traction, this book was written for you. Success in this space isn't about perfection – it's about clarity, persistence and staying connected to your purpose.

This isn't the end – it's a new beginning. Together, let's make a plan for your personal success and create the thriving, purpose-driven business (and life) you envision. You're not alone on this journey, and I can't wait to see where your next steps take you.

CHAPTER 26

IGNITE IN ACTION: HOW IT ALL COMES TOGETHER

IGNITE serves as a structured roadmap for starting and growing a successful HR consulting business. Based on my experiences and insights from coaching numerous business owners, this framework provides both the big-picture perspective and the practical steps required to build a sustainable, impactful consulting practice. With each stage of the framework – **Inspire**, **Guide**, **Niche**, **Identity**, **Team** and **Earn** – you gain clarity and confidence to navigate the complexities of consulting with purpose and success.

Inspire

- **Growth Mindset:** Cultivate a growth mindset, embracing challenges and learning from failures.
- **Psychology of Success:** Understand the psychological aspects of success, including resilience, self-motivation and emotional intelligence.
- **Consistency and Effort:** Emphasise the importance of consistent effort and perseverance in achieving long-term success.

Guide

- **Vision and Goals:** Define your long-term vision and short-term goals. Understand why you want to start a consulting business and what success looks like for you.
- **Market Research:** Identify your target market, understand their needs and analyse the competition. This will help you position your services effectively.
- **Business Plan:** Create a detailed business plan outlining your business model, services, target market, marketing strategy, financial projections and operational plan.

Niche

- **Service Definition:** Clearly define the services or products you will offer. Ensure they are structured to meet client needs efficiently and profitably.
- **Value Proposition:** Develop a compelling value proposition that differentiates your services from competitors.
- **Packaging and Pricing:** Design service packages and set pricing strategies that reflect the value you provide while being competitive and profitable.

Identity

- **Brand Identity:** Develop your brand identity, including your business name, logo and messaging that resonates with your target audience.
- **Marketing Strategy:** Create a comprehensive marketing plan, leveraging online and offline channels to attract potential clients. This can include content marketing, social media, networking and public relations.
- **Sales Process:** Develop a structured sales process to convert leads into clients. This includes lead generation, nurturing and closing strategies.

Team

- **Resourcing:** Plan for the human resources needed to scale your business, including employees, contractors and freelancers.
- **Client Services:** Build out operations to create trust and deliver valuable service to your clients.
- **Technology and Systems:** Invest in technology and systems that streamline operations and improve efficiency. Consider automation tools, CRM systems and project management software.
- **Outsourcing and AI:** Leverage outsourcing and AI solutions to handle non-core activities, allowing you to focus on strategic tasks.

Earn

- **Financial Management:** Implement sound financial practices, including budgeting, cash flow management and financial reporting.
- **Pricing Strategies:** Ensure your pricing covers costs and generates profit. Understand the financials of each service line.
- **Cost Management:** Monitor and control business expenses to maintain profitability. This includes both fixed and variable costs.
- **Risk Management:** Protect yourself, your business and team by understanding and mitigating risk..

In this chapter, we'll bring each component of IGNITE together, showing how the pieces connect and support each other to form a complete, well-rounded strategy for building a thriving HR consulting business. Whether you're just starting out or looking to refine your current business, using IGNITE as a cohesive system will help you achieve consistent growth, create value for clients and build a business that reflects your unique strengths.

INSPIRE: SETTING THE MINDSET FOR SUCCESS

The foundation of any successful business starts with the right mindset. In the **Inspire** stage of IGNITE, we emphasise developing a growth-oriented, resilient mindset that drives consistent personal and professional development.

Your mindset impacts every aspect of your business, from how you handle challenges to how you pursue opportunities. With a growth mindset (*Chapter 6: It's all in your mind: Growth versus Fixed Mindset*), you can approach each setback as a learning opportunity, staying adaptable and open to change. This mindset is reinforced by mastering the psychology of success (*Chapter 7: The Inner Game: Master the Pscyhology of Success*), which involves building resilience, self-motivation and emotional intelligence – qualities that are invaluable for any entrepreneur.

The long game (*Chapter 8: Play your Long Game, not your Short Game*) approach is also essential. Building a business is not a sprint; it's a marathon that requires commitment, patience and the ability to see beyond short-term challenges. By grounding yourself in these principles, you're setting the stage for a business that not only survives but thrives. This mindset will fuel the actions you take in the following stages, giving you the confidence and clarity to face whatever comes your way.

GUIDE: LAYING A STRONG FOUNDATION

The **Guide** stage is all about defining a clear vision and strategic direction for your consulting business. In this phase, you'll lay the groundwork by establishing your long-term goals, short-term objectives and understanding your target market.

In *Chapter 9: Dream Big, Plan Smart*, we explored the impor-tance of creating a vision that aligns with your values and goals. Knowing your "why" provides the motivation to push through challenges and remain focused on building a business that reflects your purpose. Next, in *Chapter 10: Know your Market: Clients, Competitors and Referrers*, you learned to identify and research your ideal clients, gaining insights into their needs, challenges and expectations. This understanding is crucial for building mean-ingful connections and offering services that resonate with your target audience.

Finally, in *Chapter 11: If you Fail to Plan, you Plan to Fail*, you created a detailed business plan outlining your business model, services, target market and financial projections. This blueprint serves as your compass, guiding your decisions and ensuring you're always moving toward your goals. Together, these elements give you a strong foundation and a strategic roadmap for navi-gating the complexities of running an HR consulting business.

NICHE: TURNING EXPERTISE INTO PROFIT

The **Niche** stage is where you define, refine and package your expertise into profitable, client-centered services. This is your opportunity to turn your knowledge into services that meet client needs and stand out in the marketplace.

In *Chapter 12: Define your Toolkit: Your Unique Service Offering*, you identified the core services you'll offer, structuring them in a way that provides maximum impact. Knowing exactly what's in your "toolkit" makes it easier to communicate your value and ensure your offerings are both scalable and profitable. Then, in *Chapter 13: Stand Out from the Crowd with your USP*, you developed a compelling value proposition that differentiates your business from competitors. This unique selling proposition (USP) is essential for attracting clients who resonate with your approach and see the distinct value you bring.

Pricing your services effectively is crucial, as covered in *Chapter 14: Package and Productise your Services*. By designing service packages and pricing strategies that reflect the value you provide, you ensure that every project contributes to your business's financial health. The Niche stage brings together your expertise, value and pricing, creating a foundation for a profitable consulting business that meets client needs and achieves sustainable growth.

IDENTITY: BUILDING AND SELLING YOUR BRAND

Once your services are defined, it's time to build a brand that resonates with your target audience. In the **Identity** stage, you'll create a cohesive brand that reflects who you are, what you stand for, and how you want clients to perceive your business.

In *Chapter 15: Create a Brand that Resonates and Sells*, we explored the importance of developing a brand identity, including your business name, logo and messaging. A strong brand identity helps establish credibility and sets the tone for client relationships. Next, in *Chapter 16: Your Essential Marketing Game Plan*, you learned to create a comprehensive marketing plan that includes both online and offline channels. Consistent, targeted marketing is key to keeping your brand visible and attracting leads.

Finally, in *Chapter 17: Closing the Deal: Turning Leads into Paying Clients*, we covered the essentials of a structured sales process, from lead generation to closing strategies. This process is the bridge between marketing and client acquisition, ensuring that your leads convert into loyal clients. Together, the Identity stage helps you build a brand that stands out, connects with clients and supports steady growth.

TEAM: BUILDING RESOURCES TO SCALE

In the **Team** stage, you'll focus on the people and resources needed to support and scale your business. Whether you're hiring employees, engaging contractors or using outsourced services, building a reliable team is essential for delivering high-quality work and growing sustainably.

In *Chapter 18: Engage the Right Resources for your Business*, we covered the importance of identifying the right resources, whether that's hiring, contracting or outsourcing. Each resource type has pros and cons, and choosing the right mix will depend on your business's unique needs and budget. In *Chapter 19: Deliver*

Exceptional Client Services: Building Trust and Achieving Results, we focused on what is arguably the most important aspect of building a successful HR consulting business – delivering outstanding client service. This book is designed to help you thrive as an HR consultant, and nothing drives success more than how well you serve your clients. From setting clear expectations and proactive communication to delivering consistent, high-quality outcomes, exceptional client service builds trust, strengthens relationships, and fuels referrals and long-term business growth.

Then, in *Chapter 20: Work Smarter, Not Harder with Tech*, we discussed the tech tools every consultant needs, from project management software to CRM systems and automation tools. These tools streamline operations, allowing you and your team to work more efficiently.

Finally, in *Chapter 21: The Future Is Now: Leverage AI*, we looked at leveraging AI and outsourcing for non-core activities. By integrating these solutions, you free up time and resources, enabling you to focus on strategy and client relationships. Together, these strategies give you the infrastructure and support needed to grow your consulting business without overextending yourself.

EARN: MASTERING YOUR FINANCES

Financial health is crucial to business sustainability, and in the **Earn** stage, you'll implement financial practices that keep your business profitable. This stage covers everything from setting up sound financial practices to effective pricing and cost management.

In *Chapter 22: Essential Financial Practices for Consultants*, we discussed the importance of budgeting, cash flow management and financial reporting. These practices ensure that you have a clear picture of your finances and can make informed decisions. In *Chapter 23: Profitable Pricing: Value your Value*, we explored how to set prices that reflect the value of your services while covering costs and generating profit.

In *Chapter 24: Know your Numbers: Income and Expenses*, we covered strategies for managing both fixed and variable costs. By controlling expenses and maximising profitability, you create a financially resilient business. Understanding the legalities of your business is essential for protecting your reputation, finances, and relationships. *Chapter 25: Understand and Cover the Legalities of Business* highlights key legal considerations, from contracts to compliance, helping you navigate risks with confidence.

Together, these financial practices help you maintain steady cash flow, avoid financial stress and ensure that your business is both profitable and sustainable.

IGNITE IS YOUR HR BUSINESS BLUEPRINT

Each stage of IGNITE plays a distinct role, but together, they create a cohesive, integrated approach to building a consulting business. Here's how the six pieces come together to form a complete system:

1. **Inspire** provides the mindset foundation, setting the tone for resilience and growth.
2. **Guide** creates a solid strategic base, ensuring that your business has a clear direction.
3. **Niche** allows you to turn your expertise into profitable services that meet client needs.
4. **Identity** helps you build a brand and marketing strategy that connects with clients.
5. **Team** ensures you have the right resources and technology to deliver value consistently.
6. **Earn** safeguards financial health, ensuring profitability and sustainability.

Together, IGNITE creates a balanced, structured approach to consulting. Each stage builds on the previous one, ensuring that you're not only prepared to launch but also to sustain and grow your business over time. This framework is not a one-time plan; it's a cycle you'll revisit as your business evolves, helping you stay aligned with your goals and adapt to changes in the market.

IGNITE: YOUR PATH TO SUCCESS

IGNITE offers a roadmap to success, guiding you through the complexities of consulting with confidence and clarity. As you put this framework into action, remember that it's more than just a series of steps – it's a comprehensive strategy for building a business that reflects your expertise, values and aspirations.

By following each stage of IGNITE, you'll be well-equipped to handle the challenges and seize the opportunities that come your way. This framework doesn't just guide you in building a consulting business; it empowers you to build a business that's both meaningful and financially rewarding, paving the way for lasting success.

CHAPTER 27

YOUR ACTION PLAN: IGNITE YOUR HR CONSULTING BUSINESS

My **IGNITE** framework has laid out a structured path for starting and growing your HR consulting business. Now, let's put it into action. Each section of IGNITE – **Inspire, Guide, Niche, Identity, Team** and **Earn** – contains essential steps to build a strong foundation and ensure a profitable, sustainable business.

This chapter is designed to help you take the next step by reflecting on what you've learned and translating it into a clear, actionable plan. Use the following journaling and planning questions to shape your business journey.

INSPIRE: CULTIVATING THE RIGHT MINDSET

Starting with the right mindset is essential. **Inspire** focuses on cultivating resilience, a growth mindset and an attitude of continuous learning – all necessary for the challenges ahead.

- **Why are you starting this business?** Write down your deeper motivation beyond making money – your purpose and the impact you want to make.
- **What does success look like for you in the next 12 months?** Outline your personal and professional goals for your first year using the SMART (Specific, Measurable, Achievable, Relevant, Time-bound) approach.

- **How will you stay committed to learning and growth?** List ways to expand your expertise, such as courses, books, mentors or networking events.

Action Step: Keep your purpose and goals visible to remind yourself why you started, especially on tough days.

GUIDE: LAYING A STRONG FOUNDATION

Your **Guide** stage focuses on creating a strategic foundation for your consulting business, ensuring that you have clear objectives and an understanding of your market.

- **What is your long-term vision for your business?** Use your three to five year goals to outline what success looks like and how you'll get there. Include your mission, target audience and objectives.
- **Who are your ideal clients?** Define their industry, challenges, and what they value in an HR consultant.
- **What will your business offer, and how will you structure it?** Draft a simple business plan outlining your services, pricing, and client acquisition strategy.

Action Step: Summarise your vision and business plan in a one-page document to stay focused.

NICHE: DEFINING YOUR EXPERTISE AND VALUE

The **Niche** stage is where you turn your expertise into clear, valuable services tailored to your target market. Here, you'll focus on what you offer and how you can serve clients better than anyone else.

- **What are your core services, and how do they solve your clients' biggest problems?** Write down the one to three main services you will offer.
- **What makes your business different from others?** Develop a Unique Selling Proposition (USP) that clearly communicates your expertise.

- **How can you create packaged services that provide long-term value?** Brainstorm ways to structure your services into retainer models, programs or ongoing support.

Action Step: Write your USP in one sentence and test it by explaining it to someone unfamiliar with HR consulting.

IDENTITY: BUILDING A RECOGNISABLE AND TRUSTWORTHY BRAND

With **Identity**, you'll create a brand that reflects your values and resonates with clients. A strong, consistent brand will build trust, make a memorable impact and attract the right clients.

- **What message do you want your brand to communicate?** List three words that describe your brand's personality (e.g., professional, innovative, approachable).
- **How will you ensure brand consistency?** Outline key elements such as your logo, color scheme and tone of voice.
- **What marketing activities will you focus on first?** Identify whether LinkedIn, email marketing, networking or speaking engagements will be your priority.

Action Step: Design a simple brand style guide to keep your visuals and messaging consistent.

TEAM: CREATING A SCALABLE BUSINESS MODEL

The **Team** stage helps you prepare for future growth by establishing the resources, people and systems needed to deliver high-quality work efficiently.

- **What resources do you need to deliver services?** Determine whether you'll need contractors, freelancers or technology solutions to support your services. Identify specific roles that will help you scale as you grow.
- **Which tasks take up too much of your time?** Identify work that could be automated, outsourced or assigned to a contractor.

- **What tools or technology can help streamline your business?** Research CRM systems, project management software or finance automation tools.
- **How will you document and systemise your processes?** Start outlining repeatable steps for client onboarding, invoicing and service delivery.

Action Step: Choose one system or tool to implement in the next month that will save you time or improve efficiency.

EARN: MANAGING YOUR FINANCIAL SUCCESS

In the **Earn** phase, you'll focus on keeping your business financially healthy by managing income, expenses and profitability. This ensures that your business remains sustainable and profitable.

- **What financial systems do you need to set up?** Do you have a business bank account, invoicing system and bookkeeping process in place?
- **How will you monitor cash flow?** Identify how often you'll review your income, expenses and financial reports.
- **What steps will you take to ensure profitability?** Consider whether your pricing and service packages are designed to sustain your business long-term.

Action Step: Schedule a monthly financial review to track progress, adjust pricing, and refine spending habits.

YOUR NEXT STEPS: BRINGING IGNITE TO LIFE

Now that you have reflected on each area of IGNITE, it's time to commit to action.

Which area of IGNITE do you need to focus on first?

Action Step: What is the ONE action you can take today that will move your business forward?

Your business won't grow overnight, but by taking small, consistent steps, you will build momentum and achieve real results.

Inspire

Earn

Guide

Team

Niche

Identity

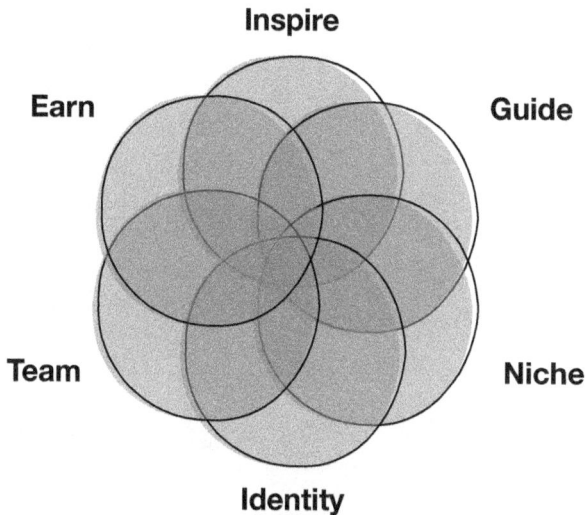

FINAL THOUGHT: IGNITE YOUR FUTURE

The journey to building an HR consulting business is filled with challenges, learning moments, and ultimately, incredible growth. Each part of IGNITE offers a pathway to confidently overcome obstacles and build a business that reflects your values, expertise and ambition. Remember, you don't have to do everything at once. Focus on steady progress, celebrate each milestone and stay committed to your vision.

As you embark on this journey, lean into the framework that has been laid out for you, but also trust your own instincts, insights and passion. You are creating something uniquely yours – a consulting business that helps clients, solves problems and makes a real impact. Embrace the process, take action and bring your vision to life. The world needs what you have to offer.

You now have the framework, insights, and tools to build a thriving HR consulting business. The only thing left to do is take action.

What will you commit to doing today, this week and this month to turn your vision into reality?

Your expertise is valuable. Your work matters. Your business has the potential to change lives.

Now is the time to IGNITE your success!

WHERE TO
FROM HERE?

As we reach the end of this book, I want to speak directly to you from the heart. Writing this has been a deeply personal journey because I have walked the very path you are now on. I've built a successful HR consulting business that has given me not only financial freedom but the balance to enjoy my family, travel extensively both locally and overseas, and live a life filled with purpose and much joy.

I share this not to impress you, but to inspire you. You can achieve this, too. I've lived IGNITE, and it has shaped not just my business but my life. But let me be real with you – there will be obstacles. Setbacks will happen. Other priorities may sometimes need to take centre stage. And that's okay. It's not a short sprint but a long, rewarding journey. What's important is to keep moving forward, even when progress feels slow. Big goals, like your BHAG (Big Hairy Audacious Goal), are achieved one step at a time.

Now, it's your turn. Take action. Dream big, be brave, be bold and remember – life is for the living. The experiences, the growth, the small victories along the way are what make this journey so worthwhile. Celebrate the small and big wins. Be grateful for each moment.

My purpose has always been about helping people make meaningful connections and contributions at work, which transpires into their personal lives. That's why I wrote this book – to help you experience the same joy and satisfaction I do in my career. I love my work, and I love helping others thrive.

Beyond business success, my journey has deeply benefited my family. It has enabled me to give my children the life I always wanted for them – a good education, meaningful opportunities, present parenting, enriching activities, quality time and memorable life experiences. While running my business has taken significant time because I've chosen to do it that way, it has also provided the flexibility to be hands-on with my children and to be there for important moments: school events, sports carnivals, debates, musical performances, tennis, netball and water polo games, and so much more. These moments, which I rarely experienced as a child, bring me immense happiness, gratitude and pride – that I've been able to provide for my children. My children are my most important job – my most significant "why", and the legacy I will leave behind one day.

Many of you are in the same situation, managing work and families. Our family, and friends, are tremendous blessings to us, a source of much happiness, but we all understand the challenge of managing the multiple conflicting priorities, and the guilt and anxiety that can come from our decisions. I wish you all the best in this and please know that I truly understand and empathise with the significance of this juggle. I really hope that my book will help you – and your families.

I would love to hear from you – my readers and fellow entrepreneurs. Share your stories, your wins, your challenges and the breakthroughs you experience along the way. Use the further reading and free resources I've included to accelerate your learning and growth. They've made a difference in my journey, and I know they will do the same for you.

Thank you for being part of my journey by reading this book. If you've found it helpful and would like to share a review, I would be exceptionally grateful. Your support means the world to me.

With love, best wishes and gratitude,

Claire

ACKNOWLEDGEMENTS

Writing this book has been an incredible journey, and I am deeply grateful to so many people who have supported, challenged and inspired me along the way.

To my early readers, Ellissa Lauder and Donna Tomasi, thank you for your invaluable feedback, honesty and encouragement. Your insights helped refine this book into something I'm truly proud of.

My first HR job was with BHP in Melbourne and was the best professional foundation I could have hoped for. That experience cemented my love for HR and prompted me to switch from an accounting to a management major in my business degree – one of the best decisions I ever made! The friendships formed in that first job remain strong to this day – Jo Cairns and Jodi Needham – thank you both.

To the many bosses and colleagues I've learned from over the years – whether through inspiration or challenge – you have all helped shape my HR and business acumen. A special thanks to Ashley Waugh and Lindsay Thorrington for believing in my potential and investing in my growth. Your faith in me made a lasting impact.

To my Harrisons team, you make me proud every day. It's an honour to work alongside such dedicated professionals. A special mention to Nea Fraser, who has been with me since the early days in my home office – you are a rock, and I appreciate you more than words can say.

To my network of fellow business owners, thank you for keeping me grounded, motivated and inspired. A special shout-out to my long-standing business coach and friend, Amanda Cole, whose wisdom and guidance have been instrumental in my entrepreneurship journey.

To Michael Hanrahan and the team at Publish Central, thank you for making the self-publishing process smooth and professional. And a special thank you to my editor, Karen Comer, for your sharp eye, patience and commitment to making this book the best it can be.

To Julia Kuris, once again thank you for your creativity and expertise in designing a cover that brings my book to life visually – I absolutely love it!

To Andrew Griffiths, your guidance once again has been a game-changer. I deeply appreciate your generosity in sharing your wisdom and experience.

To my parents, Aileen, David and Linda, thank you for your love, encouragement and support – not just of me, but of my career and family. Your belief in me has meant everything.

And finally, with the deepest gratitude, to my family – Shane, Isabel and Harry – thank you for riding this incredible rollercoaster of life with me. We've shared so many amazing moments, and I know there are many more to come. Your love, patience and support mean the world to me.

Thank you all. This book wouldn't exist without you. ♥

ABOUT THE AUTHOR

Claire Harrison was born and raised in Brisbane, and after living in Melbourne and Sydney, Claire now resides back in Brisbane with her husband and two children. She balances her career with a love for travel and family life. Her passion lies in helping others achieve professional success, particularly supporting women who aspire to start their entrepreneurial journeys while balancing family commitments.

Claire is a seasoned HR professional, entrepreneur and author with a passion for empowering others in their careers and businesses. This is her second book, continuing her commitment to sharing valuable insights with HR professionals, business leaders and aspiring entrepreneurs. Claire's first book was *The CEO Secret Guide to managing and motivating employees.*

As the Founder and Managing Director of Harrisons, established in 2009, Claire has built a respected HR consultancy known for its client-focused solutions, personalised service and professional excellence. Her extensive HR career began in the 1990s with BHP in Melbourne, and has since spanned HR leadership roles in local and global organisations.

Beyond her corporate achievements, Claire has served as a Non-Executive Director with various not-for-profit organisations, contributing her expertise to support community growth and development. She holds tertiary qualifications in Business Management, Accounting and Law and furthered her education with executive studies at Columbia Business School in New York.

LOOKING FOR MORE RESOURCES?

Make the most of what you've learned in this book with exclusive tools and templates designed to help you succeed!

- Download the Business Plan Template mentioned in the book
- Access additional resources to support your journey
- Scan the QR code or visit: www.claireharrison.co

SHARE YOUR
STORY WITH ME

Now that you've read the details of my journey and know how I built Harrisons, I'd love to hear about yours. If you take my advice and launch your own HR consulting business, share how the IGNITE framework worked for you. What changed in your life? How has your business evolved?

Your stories inspire me and others on this same journey. Please email your experiences to me at hello@claireharrison.co – I can't wait to hear from you!

WANT SOME MORE

CLAIRE HARRISON IN YOUR LIFE?

If you've got great value from Claire's latest book, there are a number of ways you can work with her. Check out the information on the following pages or visit her website at www.claireharrison.co. And of course you can connect with her on LinkedIn, Instagram and Facebook.

TURN YOUR HR CONSULTING DREAM INTO REALITY

You've finished *Start and Scale Your HR Consulting Business* – you're inspired, but let's face it: starting a business can feel overwhelming. You don't have to do it alone. Claire Harrison's Start and Scale Program gives you the tools, guidance and support you need to confidently build a thriving HR consulting business.

What you'll gain:

- Clarity: A step-by-step roadmap for starting and growing your business
- Confidence: Proven strategies for marketing, pricing and delivering your services
- Support: Monthly mentoring, a community of peers and access to exclusive events
- Online Time-Saving Tools: Ready-to-use templates, e-learning, webinars and expert guidance.

📞 Contact us today: hello@claireharrison.co

🌐 Learn more and join the program: www.claireharrison.co

ENGAGING.
INSIGHTFUL.
ACTIONABLE.

Book Claire Harrison for your Next Event

Looking for a dynamic and experienced speaker to engage, educate and inspire your audience?

Claire Harrison delivers real-world expertise and sharp insights on HR, leadership and business strategy. Whether it's a keynote, workshop or podcast, Claire's sessions are practical, relatable and results-driven – tailored to your audience's needs.

WHY BOOK CLAIRE?

✔ Expertise You Can Trust – Well over 20 years as an HR strategist and business leader
✔ Practical and Relatable – Clear, actionable strategies backed by real-world examples
✔ Future-Focused – Specialising in HR Tech, AI, Leadership and Workplace Trends.

TOPICS THAT RESONATE:

- HR Trends and AI – The future of work and leveraging technology in HR
- Leadership and Culture – Building high-performing, engaged teams
- HR for Business Leaders – Essentials for compliance, people strategy and business performance
- Entrepreneurship – Transitioning to business ownership with confidence, especially women.

WHAT PEOPLE SAY

"Claire simplifies complex HR challenges and delivers actionable insights. Her sessions are practical and inspiring."

— Event Organiser

"One of the best speakers we've had – relevant, thought-provoking and impactful."

— CEO, SME Business

LET'S MAKE YOUR EVENT A SUCCESS

Customised for conferences, workshops or panels.

- Let's talk: hello@claireharrison.co
- Learn more: www.claireharrison.co

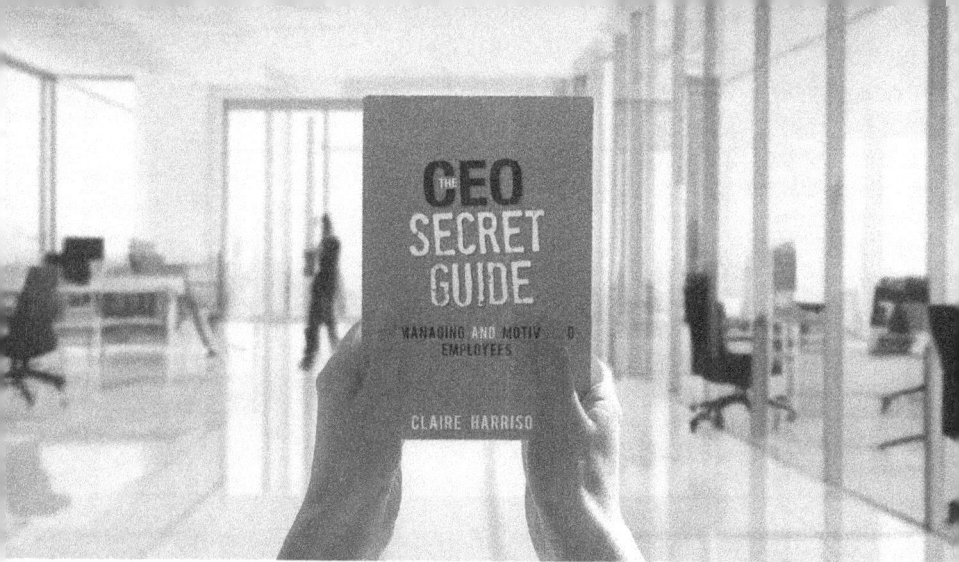

LOOKING FOR THE PERFECT GIFT FOR YOUR CEO?

If you've found the insights in this book valuable, you'll want to get your hands on my first book for your CEO – *The CEO's Secret Guide to Managing and Motivating Employees* – the essential roadmap for mastering the people side of business.

Inside, you'll discover:

✔ How to build a high-performing team that drives business growth

✔ The HR essentials every CEO needs to know to stay compliant and avoid costly mistakes

✔ Leadership strategies to engage, develop and retain top talent

✔ How to structure your business for success – from hiring to succession planning

✔ Real-world case studies and proven frameworks that simplify HR for busy business owners.

Packed with actionable insights and expert advice, this book will help you scale your business with less stress and more success.

📖 Get your copy today: hhr.com.au/product/the-ceo-secret-guide

Finally— Freedom
From HR Stress: Discover the Secret to
Effortless Team Management

Are you tired of juggling expensive consultants, confusing software, or risky DIY templates? myHRexperts combines the affordability of a template system with the expertise of a dedicated HR team—available 24/7

Tell Me More!

Are HR challenges taking over your time and energy?
Say Goodbye to HR Headaches!
Running a business is demanding – juggling operations, finances and growth while trying to stay compliant with complex HR laws can feel overwhelming. You're not alone, and you don't have to do it all yourself. At myHRexperts.com.au, we simplify HR for you, so you can focus on what you do best.

With our expert HR resources, you'll:

✔ Stay compliant with ever-changing employment laws
✔ Save time with ready-to-use HR policies, contracts and templates
✔ Prevent costly mistakes that could lead to legal risks and fines
✔ Manage your team effectively with expert guidance and best-practice strategies
✔ Feel confident knowing you have HR specialists in your corner.

What's inside?

❖ HR Templates and Policies: Instant access to legally compliant documents to protect your business
❖ Harri – Your AI Assistant: Answers your HR questions instantly – any time, day or night.
❖ Step-by-Step Guides: Easy-to-follow instructions for hiring, managing and exiting employees

- ❖ Expert Video Training: HR professionals break down complex topics into practical insights
- ❖ HR Compliance Checklist: Stay on track with easy-to-use checklists for HR compliance

Bonus: Members also receive priority access to exclusive HR webinars and discounts on consulting services!

Who is this for?

- ✔ Start-up and small business owners and managers who want simple, stress-free HR solutions
- ✔ Entrepreneurs looking to grow their team the right way
- ✔ HR professionals needing practical tools to support their business clients

www.myHRexperts.com.au

DOES YOUR BUSINESS NEED EXPERT HR SUPPORT?

Harrisons | People & Culture Specialists
⚲ **Empowering Business Leaders. Elevating Teams.**
At Harrisons, we help businesses navigate HR with confidence – ensuring compliance, streamlining operations and building high-performing teams. Whether you're an HR manager, a business owner or a CEO looking for strategic HR solutions, we're here to support you.

✔ HR Consulting and Compliance
✔ Leadership Development and Coaching
✔ Outsourced HR solutions
✔ Custom Training and Workshops
⊘ Visit us at www.hhr.com.au
📞 Let's talk HR: info@hhr.com.au

Harrisons
People • Purpose • Perform

* 9 7 8 1 9 2 3 2 2 5 8 0 0 *